GLORIA G. BOLTZ (PALMER)

I Have **Five** *Beautiful* Daughters

The Saddest Words We Ever Heard

DORRANCE
PUBLISHING CO
EST. 1920
PITTSBURGH, PENNSYLVANIA 15235

Dorrance Publishing Co
585 Alpha Drive
Pittsburgh, PA 15238
Visit our website at *www.dorrancebookstore.com*

ISBN: 978-1-6853-7228-6
eISBN: 978-1-6853-7767-0

I Have **Five**

Beautiful

Daughters

The Saddest Words We Ever Heard

Dedication

I dedicate this book to my sisters, Jewel Weeks, Judy Duncan, Dale Duncan, and Joyce Roberson who made life bearable throughout our childhood. Without my sisters to rely on and be with and laugh with and cry with, I don't believe I would be who I am today. My sisters who were my sounding boards, counselors, and prayer partners. They're the only ones who truly get it because they, too, lived it. I love them with all my heart and know I could not ask for better sisters than these.

I dedicate this book to my three sons, Charles David, Michael Bryan, and Samuel Richard who taught me more about love and family than I ever taught them. For the kind, gentle, sweet Christian men they grew up to be. My heart is full just knowing God entrusted me with three precious baby boys. And to Bryan, my husband, for working hard to always provide for me and our sons.

To my Uncle Glynn and Aunt Shirley Doyle whose selfless intercessory prayers over us five Palmer girls kept us from serious harm.

Uncle Glenn

Aunt Shirley

And I dedicate this book to God, who provided protection throughout my childhood and who has healed my spirit and heart, which has allowed me to forgive.

Gloria

Acknowledgments

I wish to thank Joyce Roberson, Dale Duncan, Mike Boltz, and Chuck Boltz, who compelled me to write this book. Who encouraged me to continue when I wanted to give up. Who had to continuously shoot down all my negativism concerning my lack of abilities and lack of education. Having no idea of how to even begin writing a book, they each made me feel like the author of a best seller even before I typed the first word onto a blank page. I'm sure without that kind of encouragement, I would have given up.

I wish to thank my husband, Bryan, for putting up with my plugging away at a keyboard for five months without complaining and often preparing his own meals.

I wish to thank my sweet Granny, Aunt Mae, and Aunt Emmie, who fed me many times as a child. I probably never even said thank you to them, but I am truly grateful. They're all with Jesus now, but in God's timing I shall thank them all in person.

I wish to thank my beautiful aunt Shirley Doyle, who has shown me the power of prayer and what the epitome of a Christian and a gentle spirit looks like.

I wish to thank Vincent Griffin and Ivy Walters for the protection they provided and for being there for scared little girls.

I love each and every one of you and pray God's blessings upon you all.

Gloria

Foreword

When I think about mercy, I think about pain. Whether you are experiencing pain or trying to think about how you may be causing others' pain, whether you mean to or not, pain can sear the mind and/or soul. It's obviously very prevailing. What astounds me and inspires me simultaneously is how in spite of what could overwhelm the senses can be not only relegated to something trivial, but channeled into positive energy to stop similar cycles. People wrong each other all the time. If asked in an honest forum, there may be some sadistic individuals who actually intend to wrong others, but I'm more inclined to believe that when it happens, it's an unintended consequence: be it misunderstanding, misplaced rage, lack of knowing how to process one's environment. For whichever of the aforementioned reasons, it obviously happens.

What is amazing to me, and quite honestly something that truly warms my heart is when someone can resist the urge to respond in kind, and thereby cancel the cycle. Without abusing the soapbox, I would simply suggest that Jesus told us to "turn the other cheek." Do not repay unkindness with unkindness. I could have any mother, any father, any physical impairment, any economic outlook…but what I couldn't be guaranteed is what I got. A warm home, a hot meal every night, a hug when I needed it, a friend when I needed it most, an advocate…and most importantly… someone who SHOWED me Jesus, not just did Him lip service.

Mathematically, the odds of having been born into a free nation, a warm home, a place where I don't have to fear deadly disease or invaders is kind of low…so I won life's lottery by blind luck. I won't tell you the end of the story; only God can do that. But I will tell you it's good. As a youngster, I watched in mystery as I witnessed my mom and dad and two of her sisters embark on a mission to repaint, restore, and buy furniture/knickknacks, etc., things that just make a home a home for my mom's parents. It was just another visit with the family to me at the time. But what I later learned is that it was a concerted and planned effort to show my grandparents charity, love, and forgiveness that I only hope one day to be capable of and understand. This is Christ.

Chuck Boltz

Introduction

This story is told from the memories of Gloria, the fourth daughter of Ed and Lorraine Palmer. It is from her perspective and not intended to hurt or embarrass anyone. The bad language used is relevant to the story and has been omitted or cleaned up where possible.

The purpose in writing the story of the five Palmer girls' childhood, besides being asked to by my sisters and sons on many occasions, but more importantly to show the power of prayers. Looking back, I am convinced that without the intervention and Holy protection of God almighty, horrible things would have happened to us all. Being totally neglected, unwanted, unfed, and left to fend for ourselves, there were angels all around, unbeknownst to us at the time. And also, to be an encouragement to others who were raised by abusive or neglectful parents. As an adult, it is your choice to refuse to repeat the patterns of abuse upon your own children. And finally, to enlighten those who thought they knew the five Palmer girls, who had a preconceived opinions based on outward appearances.

I hesitated for the past fifty years to write this book

for fear of dishonoring my parents. But after much soul searching, prayers, and prompting from others, I realized that I did not create my parents' reputations; they did. If anything, they tarnished our reputations all because of the powerful demonic vice of alcohol.

Chapter 1

Some folks began their story with, "I was born at a very young age" and of course that's a given, but I cannot remember a time when I didn't feel like a grown-up. That was true for me and I'm sure for my four sisters also. There were many, many times we had to be the adults in our family from as far back as I can remember.

Born and raised in Augusta, Georgia, my mama, Marian Lorraine Hall McDonald Palmer, as she liked to refer to herself, was the fourth of eight children, six girls and two boys. Elizabeth, Mae, Edna, Lorraine, Junior, Betty, Raymond, and Beatrice Hall.

Her mother, Mama Hall (Lucille), was a mean old hellraiser and I believe Satan himself looked up to her. Mama said that Mama Hall had eighteen children in total, two sets of twins and two sets of triplets that were either stillborn or died shortly after birth and only the eight single births survived. (I wish now I had enough sense to check into that story while some of my maternal aunts were still living, since my mama teetered between delusional and a pathological liar.) But either way, it's safe to say out of those eight single births, my mama was the one to inherit that hellraiser "attribute." At least she thought of it as an attribute and she was proud of it. She also was the prettiest of the six girls growing up and she knew it.

Augusta Georgia is known mostly for the Masters Golf Tournament and Fort Gordon Military base. Mama, at the age of sixteen met and married Fred McDonald, a soldier, who was about twenty-three years old. He was a gambler and a heavy drinker. He was booted out of the Army with a dishonorable discharge after being AWOL for quite some time. Fred died of tuberculosis one year and four months after they married and Mama was the sole beneficiary of Fred's life insurance. She purchased two separate gravesites at the local cemetery, each consisting of eight graves. And because she was under age, they were purchased in her daddy's name, Milton Ivy Hall. She moved back in with her parents and had enough insurance money left over to set Granddaddy up with a bicycle repair shop; she bought her parents some home furnishings as well. Up until then, her parents barely scraped together a living raising chickens and odd jobs. To say they were poor would be an understatement! Life was a little easier with the money Granddaddy made repairing bicycles, but not by much. They still raised chickens and ate a lot of eggs, I'm sure. Granddaddy later got a job working at the ice house where ice was cut into blocks to be sold to folks who used an "Ice Box" rather than a refrigerator.

My daddy, Edward L. Palmer, was also born and raised in Augusta, Georgia. He was the eldest of six kids. It was said his mother, Murt Jenkins, (we called her Granny), gave birth to him at the age of thirteen and she would be outside playing with other kids while his grandmother took care of him. He never had a full-blooded sibling, and he never knew his daddy while he was growing up. Granny later had two more sons, David and Herbert by her second husband, last name King. I don't believe they ever knew their daddy while growing up either. She then had four daughters by her third husband, Carl Jenkins. Elizabeth, Emmie, Shirley, and Carlene Jenkins. Carlene died when she was about six months old. Granny says she put the baby in between them in their bed because it was too cold in the house. Carl was drunk and rolled over on top of the baby during the night and the baby was dead when they woke up. (It was written up as Crib Death.) Daddy always said his grandmother raised him, so I do not know at what age he went to live with his mama and Carl Jenkins. But his grandmother is the one who taught him about the Lord. Daddy always had a very strong belief in the bible and believed it was the sovereign word of God throughout his entire life.

Carl Jenkins did not want his stepsons, Murt's three boys, living with them and he was extremely mean and

My Mama   My Mama's Parents

Mama at Fred's gravesite   Fred McDonald

hateful to them. He was even mean and hateful to his own three daughters, according to Aunt Shirley. She said he would beat the tar out of them if they did anything wrong, and the only time he had ever shown any kindness toward them was in his old age where he could no longer do for himself and he depended on their help for his every need.

Carl was an ole' mountaineer from Waynesboro, North Carolina who was the first born to his mother, and I'm pretty sure he never knew his real daddy. His mother married and had ten more children, nine boys and one girl. The family owned and ran Apple Orchards, so there was always plenty of work to do, no doubt, but I'm not sure if Carl was part of that. He wasn't wanted there by his stepdad, who was extremely abusive toward him. So, Carl lived with and was raised by his grandparents.

At some point, most likely during his teen years, Carl made his way to Augusta, Georgia/ South Carolina area to work in the cotton mills. One would think, being so mistreated by his own stepfather that Carl would not want to inflict that same harsh meanness upon his own stepchildren. He had to know what it felt like to be so unloved and unwanted and yet he grew up to repeat that behavior as a stepfather. (I will never understand how so many folks who suffered so much pain as children, grow up to be the source of that same kind of pain for their own children or stepchildren. I would think they would be the last people to do such things.)

My granny also worked in the cotton mills, so I'm guessing that's how she met Carl Jenkins. She walked with an extreme limp due to one of her legs being several inches shorter than the other. She did a sort of rocking side to side motion when she walked. I'm sure that had to be painful at times. It sure looked painful. I never asked her about it because I thought she was born that way and didn't want to embarrass her. But actually, she got her leg or hip caught in a Warper machine while working in the cotton mill. It was very traumatic and she endured a lot of painful therapy. She was hospitalized for nine months due to the severity of her injury. I don't know if this happened before or after she had her daughters with Carl, but I'm sure she already had her three sons. I've never heard Granny complain about her discomfort or about anything for that matter.

We found out years later, she loved to go in a car. She and Carl never owned a car and although folks popped in to see them, they didn't necessarily offer to take her some place. That broke my heart to know she wanted to get out and about and yet I never knew that. (She never asked and never complained, at least that I'm aware of.) She was a kind and very soft-spoken lady and I loved her dearly; we all did. I've never heard anyone ever say a bad word about her, (other than my mama) so if she had any flaws, we never knew about them. Now, she did—later on in life after all her kids were grown and gone—like to take a little nip. She'd get a little tipsy, but she never drank enough to allow it to interfere with her finances or her conducting everyday life. She made her bed every single morning without fail, she cooked breakfast and dinner every day and always washed up her dishes. She was a good house-keeper and always wore a dress and an apron. (And she loved the TV show *Gunsmoke*.)

Poor Uncle Herbert would hide under their house for days on end to keep from being beat by Carl. No matter the weather, how cold or how hot, Herbert was afraid to go back in the house. Carl hated Herbert the most out of his three stepsons, I'm told, because Herbert would sass and argue back to Carl where David was shy and more withdrawn and more obedient. But Carl finally told my daddy and David they had to go; he wasn't feeding them anymore and since they had no place to go, they each lied about their age and joined the service.

This is the house (center) at 1844 Green Street, where daddy was living with Carl and Granny and his five siblings. The house Herbert squatted under for hours on end to escape Carl's wrath. These houses are called shotgun houses because they are just three rooms straight through. They consisted of two rooms, then the kitchen if you can call it that. It had a sink attached to the wall, so it was intended to be the kitchen and you had to supply everything else. The front and middle rooms were usually used for bedrooms because most folks had several kids if not an entire shebang, so there was never a "living room." There were no closets in these houses, or if there was, it was only a very small one, so everything was stored in dresser drawers. Most had an "outhouse" rather than indoor toilets in those days. It made for a whole lotta fun!

Carl and Granny

Chapter 2

My daddy joined the Marines at the age of seventeen in 1940. Not sure which branch Uncle David joined, but he was younger than Daddy. Daddy was sent to Pearl Harbor and was there when Hawaii was attacked in December 1941. He went through a lot over there and witnessed a lot; I assume that because he would never talk about it. That subject was strictly off-limits with him and when he finally came back to the States, he was totally committed to serving the Lord and becoming a preacher. So, I'm guessing he did a lot of praying and deal-making with God, fearing he would never come home alive. Aunt Shirley just recently validated my theory when she told me that Daddy once mentioned to her and Granny, concerning his experience in Pearl Harbor, that he greatly feared for his life. He had slid in the mud down into a ditch or embankment and his clothes caught on a branch or some roots making him a sitting duck for being shot. And he did indeed make an agreement with God to serve Him always if he could just make it out of there alive. (I guess I'm a good guesser!)

None of us five daughters ever heard the story of how Daddy and Mama met, but they were a beautiful couple. He always dressed in a suit and tie, she in her heels, a pretty dress, makeup, and she always had a ribbon or a bow in her hair. They went all over Augusta, on foot, to the movies, visiting folks and just holding hands while strolling around. Daddy said she was so beautiful and funny back then. She kept him laughing and she turned heads everywhere they went. He was proud as a peacock to have her on his arm. I never knew that side of her and certainly never knew she had a sense of humor. The Mama I knew didn't joke, didn't sing, didn't dance, and she almost never laughed. Even while others were laughing and cutting up, she was pretty much stone-faced. (She was always as serious as a bomb threat.)

Ed and Lorraine Palmer

985 Broad Street, Mama and Daddy rented an apartment over this business place downtown on their wedding day. Friday March 16, 1945.

They married when she was eighteen and he was twenty-one, I believe. (Although her marriage license to Fred McDonald says she was eighteen then too, so who knows her real age!)

They had their first daughter ten months later and had moved into this historic Ezekiel Harris house, which at that time was a boarding house. The house is now 224 years old and still stands today as a museum. It stood empty and in disrepair for many years and eventually was purchased by the city and restored and staged with furnishings from the 1700s to 1800s time period, and they now give tours on Saturdays.

My sister Jewel said she was told Uncle Herbert stayed with Mama and Daddy in the Ezekiel Harris house to get away from Carl. The only place they had for Uncle Herbert to sleep was on a cot and they had to place it against the door. But every morning when they woke up, the cot would be moved with Uncle Herbert still in it and the door would be open, supernaturally.

Built in 1797 Ezekiel Harris House is said to be "the finest eighteenth-century house surviving in Georgia. Located at 1822 Broad Street. It was already 148 years old when my parents lived here. It is now an Augusta Historic Museum. It was all white back then and was said to be haunted. My parents said they heard chains rattling during the night. Also said whenever it rained, a little girl would stand outside the door of their bedroom knocking and crying "Mama." When they opened the door, no one was there, but there would be a puddle of water on the floor and only in front of their door.

I don't know what Daddy did for a living in the beginning of their marriage, but after they had their first daughter, Jewel, and while she was still a baby, they moved to Nashville, Tennessee so Daddy could attend Trevecca Nazarene Bible College.

My parents never really had conversations with us girls about much of anything, so I'm not exactly sure how that all worked. Daddy went to Trevecca Bible College on a GI bill, but I wondered if that included transportation to Nashville or if someone, a friend of Daddy's maybe, drove them to Nashville and introduced them to and set them up to live with the lady they stayed with there. I wonder now if the GI bill included any money, like for a food allowance. Who knows, no one left to ask, but while in Nashville, they had two more daughters, Judy and Dale. The entire four years they were in Nashville, Daddy rode a bicycle everywhere he went or he walked. Good thing my mama was the homebody type since she had three baby daughters, no transportation, and certainly didn't know her way around.

They moved back to Augusta in late 1950 or early 1951. My parents and sisters moved into the Project for low-income folks. (Some folks referred to it as The Projects, but more commonly called Ohmstead Homes) and shortly afterwards I was born, (mid-March).

Daddy didn't have a church to preach in and would go to people's homes to hold a bible study or a little preaching service for them. Maybe it was for older folks who couldn't get out much. He was a guest preacher in churches at times where he also played the guitar and sang. He was an enthusiastic preacher with a lot of "fresh out of bible college biblical knowledge" yet immature and uncouth enough to believe if he beat folks over the head with the word, he could save their souls. Mama said more than once that if relatives seen Daddy coming, they would lock their doors! Not sure exactly when it was he gave up or how long he attempted to be a preacher, but without his own church to pastor, he certainly could not make a living by doing it the way he was doing it. And by mid-1953 and while still living in the project, their fifth daughter was born and how on earth they made a living is beyond me!

This was long before there was any such thing as welfare and food stamps. I can tell you, the relatives on either side of the family were in no financial position to help them. Some say Mama worked in one of the cotton mills for a while. If she did, she would've had to walk there and leave four kids alone, one being a newborn and the oldest being six. Or if it was after the birth of the fifth daughter, the oldest would've been eight and one newborn. I cannot fathom entrusting an eight-year-old with a newborn, but even more than that, I cannot fathom my mama working a job! She would've been done slapped somebody! She hated leaving the house, she pretty much hated people and everything and everyone got on her last nerve! (Her words, not mine.) But finally, Daddy started driving a taxicab during this time hoping it would be just until he could pastor a church. He also received a monthly check of a whole whopping $19 from the military from the wounds he suffered at Pearl Harbor.

Just as a footnote—I would like to set straight a story that was told long and wrong for many years. It was said Daddy was wounded by shrapnel, and when it was removed from his body, he had it made into a bracelet for Mama. Two hearts connected on top with a one-inch band from either side which curved around to an open end. It was all one solid silver-looking piece that slid onto the side of the wrist then around. Daddy walked around the house bare-chested and in shorts many times through the summers. He had no scars at all on his back, his chest, his belly, or legs. The only scar he had was on his one thigh where, while in the military, his middle and ring fingers were surgically separated and they grafted the skin off his thigh to cover his inner fingers. He had what is called syndactyly, a condition where a person is born with their fingers and or toes fused together, sometimes called webbed. He had that on one hand and both feet. Just the two toes next to his big toe were fused together but only halfway up, so those would definitely be considered webbed toes. It was said he had the bracelet made in Hawaii but he didn't even meet Mama until he returned to Augusta from the Marines.

He may have brought back a piece of shrapnel as a souvenir and later had it made into a bracelet. The bracelet was engraved with his and her names and a date. I wish it was still in the family so I could read the date. But more likely than not, it was an anniversary gift to Mama he had engraved on a bracelet he came across in a souvenir shop in Nashville. Mama always had a fictional "story" to go with everything. His "wound" in the military was shell-shocked. (Psychological disturbance caused by prolonged exposure to active warfare, especially being under bombardment.) We witnessed signs of Daddy being shell-shocked a few times as the years went on, but he was never wounded with shrapnel in Pearl Harbor unless it was in his buttocks. I will admit, I've never seen his bare rump to know if there's a scar there!

For however long my daddy was a preacher, he did finally give up. Not only did no one want to hear his overzealous hellfire and brimstone sermons, but Mama would never attend any of his services or bible studies. She drank a lot and constantly made accusations of what he was really up to when he went to church or held bible studies. She was extremely jealous of him and claimed he was only going to church to meet women. He never said "when" this happened, but he did say the last time he preached in a church back then, Mama came in drunk, walked right down the center aisle, cussing and accusing. She had a half pint of liquor stuck in her bra protruding up very obvious from her blouse. She began yelling, "Okay, which one of these bitches are ya here for? I know damn well you're whoring around with one of 'em!" He said he had to leave the podium and force her out the door with her cussing and yelling the whole way out! They went home where he cried and cried then decided to get drunk with her! He said he felt as though all the forces of hell came against him and it seemed no amount of prayers or talking to her ever made any difference.

See, us kids always thought he turned her into a drunk. We thought that was the reason her parents couldn't stand him; in fact, most of her family didn't like him. Not sure what was said over the years or by whom, but we always had the impression HE was the drunk who took her down a slippery slope with him. Only years and years later after we were all grown did Mama's brothers say she was an alcoholic when he married her! Daddy didn't realize it at the time, but she became an alcoholic while married to Fred McDonald. He probably knew she drank, but didn't know she was an alcoholic. She kept it under control enough in the beginning, but over time she drank more and more.

In fact, my sister Judy always said, speaking of Mama, "Ad damn, I'd drink too if I was married to a sorry-ass drunk like Ed Palmer, who wouldn't work and if I had five hungry kids to feed with no money coming in!" So, I guess between Judy saying those things and Mama not being truthful, we grew up thinking Daddy was the instigator in all that.

The house they all lived in for the 4 yrs in Nashville at 408 43rd Ave

Daddy said every time they looked around, Jewel and Judy went missing. They always knew exactly where to find them, though, on the front porch of the neighbor's house, rocking!

This is the lady who took them into her home

This picture was taken of Jewel, Judy and Dale shortly before leaving Nashville.

Chapter 3

In the early years of our childhood, others have since told us that Mama took care of us kids and we always looked fairly nice. She tried to acquire clothing for us and bathe us and brushed our hair and made sure we ate. I'll have to take their word for that because I was young enough that I don't remember that Mama. Jewel said they even got Easter baskets sometimes. I only remember ever getting one Easter basket, but I don't remember what age I was and even then, the Easter baskets were free, given out at some church. I have prayed many times, "God, if there are any good virtues my mama had while we were growing up, please let me remember them. Please bring to my remembrance things about my mama that I can be proud of or at least remember fondly." I still occasionally pray that and hope something pops in my mind, but so far nothing.

Jewel tells me while living here in the project that she witnessed Mama lying out in the grass screaming and yelling. Aunt Mae's husband came out and picked Mama up and carried her into the house. No doubt

Mama was half lit and looking for male attention. Even if she had to get it from her brother-in-law.

We lived here for the first two to three years of my life, and from then on, I had a reoccurring nightmare most of my life. It was very short but dramatic to me. In the nightmare I am looking through bars while lying on my right side. I can see a doorway across the room that seemed so far away, as though the room I'm in is very large. I see a pair of legs and two arms very suddenly appear and bounding into the room toward me. The arms are bent at the elbow with the forearms straight out and fists shaking up and down. The arms and legs come closer and closer, then I wake up with my heart racing. This nightmare happened at the very least two to three times a month if not more and it never deviated one iota, always the same exact scenario.

Daddy, over a period of sixteen years, drove a cab off and on. (Just as a footnote: My guess is he started driving a cab as soon as he got out of the Marines and that's how he met Mama. And I'm guessing this is a good guess since I'm such a good guesser! LOL!!!)

During our childhood, he would drive for the Dixie Cab Co. in Augusta, get fired, drive for the Fleming Cab Co., get fired, drive for Checker Cab Co., get fired, back to the Dixie Cab, get fired… all to do with drinking. He would get drunk and not show up for days and, of course, they would fire him. So, he would go to the other cab company. He was fired for the same reasons

The Projects: We lived at 2164 C Street. I'm the newborn.
I wish I could remember this Mama.

with all three of them, back and forth. He wrecked a couple cabs too. He would get drunk while out there driving, and at least once he walked away after rolling up over a curb leaving the driver's door wide open and the front of the cab part way up on the sidewalk! Just walked away… or rather staggered away.

They always hired him back when he sobered up and wanted to come back. After all, most of the cab drivers, at least back then, were in the same class as him, DRUNKS. Daddy said he had lots of regulars who would specifically request Ed Palmer by name when they called for a cab. He kept them laughing (when he was sober). He loved to cut up and tell jokes and was very easy to talk to. So, it was a ride plus entertainment! I can't even picture Daddy picking up a fare and dropping them off without engaging them in a hilarious conversation. He was very likable and most folks loved talking with him. (Just as long as he wasn't preaching at folks.)

Jewel was telling me she remembers when Edna Eubanks, whose brother was married to Daddy's sister, and lived a few doors down from us, use to let her window up a bit so that Jewel and Judy could stand outside and watch and hear her television through the window. They weren't allowed inside because her husband, who was always half drunk and lying on the couch, was mean and would never stand for it. Mama and Daddy didn't have a TV at the time.

After moving from the project, where I have no memories of my childhood whatsoever, we moved to a house on Harper Street, according to my oldest sister's recollection. I have no memories at that address either. Then we moved to the 1900 block of Broad Street where I turned four years old and there's where I have my first memories. It was of my youngest sister, Joyce, being hit by a car the night before she turned two. The newspaper article in the *Augusta Chronicle* reads as follows...

Augusta Chronicle
July 30, 1955
Saturday
2- year-old girl struck by car
A 2-year old girl was dragged 75 feet Friday night

after being struck by an automobile on the 1900 block of Broad Street, Patrolman J.J. Culpepper reported.

The child, Joyce Palmer, daughter of Mr. and Mrs. Edward Palmer of 1921 Broad Street, was admitted to the University Hospital with a fractured left leg and possible head injuries. Her condition was listed as fair.

Culpepper said the girl toddled into the path of an automobile driven by Joseph Abrams, 26, of Evans, Ga. He was technically charged with reckless driving.

We lived in unit 1921 and there were no green doors back then and the railing on the porches was made of wood. There were two narrow lanes in either direction, no turning lanes.

When I read that article from the newspaper archives, I felt so sorry for the man charged, Joseph Abrams. Broad Street was a very busy street during the 1950s and 1960s, and there's no way he would've seen such a tiny child who was stooping down and then started coming into his lane with so much traffic all around him. He was only twenty-six years old and I've often wondered what this did to him emotionally also. It really wasn't his fault....

Seems each sister has a little different memory of what actually happened that night. But all agree on the fact that each sister ran down the steps, out of our house (actually more of an apartment unit) and right across the street to Tuten's Grocery Store to buy Joyce something for her birthday. Don't have a clue how much money each of us or they received, but supposedly Mama gave them or us each something to go to the store. Jewel then Judy went down the stairs and darted across the street, followed by Dale. I don't think I went, but I may have. That part doesn't come back to me. They or I left the door standing open and two-year-old Joyce crawled down the steps and followed. That's when she went out into the busy street and got hit by the car.

Judy claims she saw what she thought was a little dog in the street and was calling to it in fear of it being run over. Joyce had long hair then and she was in a squatting position in the middle of the road between the lanes so she looked more like a small animal than a baby. My daddy's Aunt Mame lived two doors down from Tuten's Store and she saw or heard the commotion. She later spread the rumor that Mama was upstairs with a man and wanted the kids out of there for a while.

Mama claimed he was a TV repairman (and yes, he came out on a Friday night to fix her TV, and yes, my daddy was in the VA hospital at the time!) Truth be told, the TV repairman was probably the one who gave the kids money to leave the house. I can't imagine Mama having any spare money, no matter how small the amount was. Or affording a TV repairman! Looking back, I believe Aunt Mame may have been correct about the man in our house. Because Mama had zero income to live on; she didn't work; Daddy was in the VA hospital having all his teeth pulled, and she was never the type to give a flip about our birthdays.

My sister Dale, who would've been six at the time, says Aunt Mame and her adult daughter, Charlotte, both grabbed Dale and took her inside their house and tied her to a chair. They had a black Chihuahua that barked constantly while Dale cried and yelled and begged to be let loose. The dog yelped continuously in that high pitch *Arf, Arf, Arf, Arf, Arf,* which further escalated Dale's anxiety. She felt completely traumatized knowing her baby sister was just hit by a car and here she was tied to a chair inside someone's home she vaguely knew with a crazed dog wanting to attack her! When Dale recalls the events of that night now, she can't believe anyone could be so cruel as to tie her to a chair considering what was taking place. She hated them both and she still hates Chihuahuas. Every time anyone in the family brings up the time Joyce was struck by a car, Dale starts telling what happened to "her" that night and everyone says, "Poor Dale" while Joyce looks at everyone in total astonishment that Dale is the one getting all the sympathy. Then we all laugh.

My only recollection of my baby sister being hit by a car starts afterwards. I remember walking across a big field, which was probably a grassy vacant lot, and Mama was holding my hand. I can see she's wearing white sandals and I keep looking down because I can feel stickers in my feet. I don't remember if I was barefoot or maybe wearing sandals also, but I remember the stickers pricking my feet. Either way I never felt that close to my mama again, but I'll always remember her holding my hand as we walked from our house to the University Hospital to see Joyce. I don't remember whether any of my sisters were with us or not, just Mama holding my hand.

This was several days after the accident, so maybe school was back in session and my other three sisters may have been in school that day. In the hospital room, I remember seeing Joyce in a crib, her leg in a cast and her other leg in a half cast. There was a bar between her legs connecting one casts to the other. There was a piggy bank in her crib that I believe one of the nurses gave her or maybe a relative; it was a miniature milk jug with a lock and key on the side near the top.

The piggy bank was like this one.

There was a doll; I believe it was a Raggedy Ann and a small plastic guitar in her crib also. Don't have a clue who brought those in for her.

My next memory was while sitting on our front porch, seeing Daddy come walking up the sidewalk toward us after being released from the Linwood Hospital. We ran toward him saying, "Daddy, Daddy, Joyce got ran over." He said in a very low and sad voice, "I know it."

Thank the Lord it was no worse than it was and she eventually was good as new. My sisters tell me that they would drag Joyce all over the house and even down the stairs by holding on to that bar that was between the leg casts. Joyce loved it and would laugh as if she was on an amusement ride.

Even though I have no memory of leaving the house the night Joyce was run over, I may have. It would "somewhat" explain why Mama hated me so much. If I did indeed go to Tuten's store with my sisters, I would've been the last one to leave the house, the one to leave the door open. Joyce wasn't big enough to reach the doorknob and open the door herself. It would've been my fault. Maybe after hearing it was "Gloria's fault" I blocked it from my memory. I can only imagine the words that came out of Mama's mouth. But I'm only speculating here. Or another good guess!

Chapter 4

From there we moved to Tuttle Street. Our house was at the top of the hill on the left. Those houses are all torn down now and even that part of the street is gone!

We moved with the help of a friend of Daddy's (or Mama's) named Cottonbird. He had a truck and they asked him to move us. I vaguely remember what Cottonbird looks like except he had a large nose that was flat on top and bent to one side and dirty blond hair. He was an ugly old cuss to say the least. Well, they got a kitchen table and chairs, a mattress, and us kids in the back of the pickup on the first load to Tuttle Street before they decided to get drunk instead of finish moving. Evidently somewhere along the route, they stopped and got some moonshine. They called it Home Brew and there were a couple boxes there in the floor with jars of moonshine in them. It was another "shotgun" house and the mattress was on the front room floor.

We had nothing, NOTHING to eat in the house, not even a refrigerator or stove yet. We had not eaten in Lord knows when, Dale and Joyce and I got some of that moonshine and drank it. Of course, with empty stomachs and never having drank before, it would've only taken one good swallow till we were all as drunk as they were. Dale and I put Joyce in one of the boxes the moonshine had been in and was attempting to carry her in it. We tripped over the mattress and dropped her. The room wasn't a whole lot bigger than the mattress, and luckily, she landed on the mattress! We laughed and laughed and we all three lay down on that mattress because the room was spinning around. I vaguely remember Granddaddy and Mama Hall and Uncle Junior showing up!

I remember the three of them standing in the kitchen where my mama and daddy and Cottonbird were seated at the table, the only other things they had brought in that day. Uncle Junior was hollering at them, mostly at my daddy, and that's what made us go to the kitchen. Junior hauled off and popped my daddy's face! Then they made us three kids get in their car. I don't recall where Jewel and Judy were, but they weren't there. They probably had gone to an aunt's house. I remember looking out the back window of Uncle Junior's car and seeing my daddy standing out on the sidewalk looking at us being driven away. He looked so sad, his hair all sticking straight up and wall-eyed drunk; he was waving to us. We were all crying, "Please don't leave my daddy." The three of them in the car ignored us girls and were angrily talking about Mama and Daddy amongst themselves. Talking about what low-down sorry asses our parents are and how we should all be taken away from them. Of course, they had no interest in taking us in permanently; they thought we should be made wards of the state.

They took us to Mama Hall's where she promptly put us in the tub and bathed us. (I can only imagine how we looked and smelled since all five if us girls wet the bed and slept together, or at least three in one bed and two in the other. We didn't own a washing machine and had just a few raggedy clothes, which we slept in). Mama Hall put a man's white T-shirt on each of us, which fit us more like a dress, and put whatever we were wearing in her washing machine. We wondered if we were gonna get to keep those "dresses!" But no such luck...she made us a banana sandwich. I don't recall whether she gave us anything to drink or not. (A banana sandwich is where ya mash up a banana with a fork; sprinkle white granulated sugars on top, then stir briskly till it becomes sorta slimy. Good stuff! It's even better over buttered toast but she just put it on white bread.)

After we were through eating our banana sandwich, Joyce and I knelt down in front of her front-loading washing machine. We had never seen anything like that before! We could see white soap bubbles through the machine's "window" and watched in amazement at how the more it flipped and flopped the more and more suds it made until the entire window turned white wid'em. (She must've used a LOT of soap in an attempt to remove all the smell and filth.) It was as good as watching television to us, and when it went into a spin cycle, we thought our clothes disappeared! We were looking into a black hole with no suds or clothes in sight! We said things to one another like, "Wut happened to our clothes?"

"Mama Hall, Mama Hall, our clothes are all gone!" No one answered us or remarked on our curiosity. Finally, the machine stopped the spin cycle and began to fill with rinse water. We were absolutely glued to that washing machine's window! "There's our clothes! Our clothes are back in it!!!"

"Wut's it gonna do na-uh?"

"I don't know!"

"Where's the wringer rollers at?"

"I don't know!"

"Are we gonna have to wring'em out wid our hands?"

"I don't know!" We were going back and forth asking and answering one another. Our questions went unanswered by Mama Hall, but we didn't care... we're gonna watch and see what happens next! But Mama Hall just ignored everything we asked and made us go lay down on some pallets she'd made on the floor to sleep on. Don't know if she owned a dryer but the next day our clothes were dry and she put them on us and Junior drove us home. I don't remember her giving us anything else to eat that morning. Junior lectured Mama and Daddy and drove off. Mama Hall was not kind or gentle or sympathetic in any way towards us. She was gruff and mean and sarcastic and seemed to be mad at the world that she had to even be bothered with us. And Uncle Junior was just like her, mean as hell. I now believe they come got us more to spite Mama and Daddy than any concern for our well-being. They never hugged us or asked questions on how often we ate or how long Mama and Daddy had been drunk.

We were telling Mama all about this "Mo-sheen" that washes yo clothes fa'ya! She mumbled something like, "Who cares what dem sums-a-bitches have."

I believe it was during this time, or else it was on Harper Street where I have no memory of living, but Dale was only about five years old. A man was at the house that Mama and Daddy vaguely knew, probably some drunk Daddy dragged in and he was gonna go to the store for something. He asked Mama could he take Dale with him. I assume he was buying them something alcoholic because she didn't have a problem with it. Heck, she probably figured that's insurance that he will come back! So, this man drives Dale out into the woods and parked. He opened the glove compartment and takes out a picture of a naked little girl and asked Dale if she looks like that?

Dale was so embarrassed she covered her face up with her hands. The man got out of the car and removed the back seat and laid it on the ground. He no more than did that when they heard a family coming through the woods, so he quickly tossed the seat back in the car and drove off and took her home. She cannot remember whether or not he ever stopped at a store. He most likely dropped her off and kept going in fear she'd say something about what he did. But Mama would've been more upset that the man didn't come back than what he attempted to do to Dale and that's not a guess! But once again we can see where God's protection was on us.

We did not live on Turtle Street long. Usually, the length of time spent in any one house all depended on how tolerant the rent man was. He'd be given a but-tload of excuses and a time they "might" be able to pay something toward the rent. We soon found out having five daughters became their biggest asset since land-lords were reluctant to set folks out on the street with five little ones, especially in the winter months. I truly believe that's about the only reason Mama didn't give us up to a children's home. That and the fact her mentality was, "Ain't no damn body gonna tell Lorraine what to do! By God, those are my damn young'uns."

From there I believe we moved to Pearl Ave. The units on Pearl Ave. were pretty much like the units we lived in on Broad Street, all connected like one very long building with porches. No doubt they were built by the same builders and probably owned by the same people or company.

Pearl Ave

The only resemblance to these units now from when we lived there is they're all still connected. Back then, they were all wood, not bricked, had individual porches, lousy windows, and doors. I believe we lived in the one more toward the far end. Maybe even all the way to the end or close to it.

Although I was still very little, I remember several things from this address. I believe I was five years old when we lived here, Joyce would've been three then, Dale seven, Judy nine and Jewel ten or eleven.

Some of us kids were standing on the side porch with Mama and a man was there that she was talking to. Possibly an insurance man or such, since back then door to door salesmen were common. She was about half drunk and trying to act all cool and she crossed her legs, propping one foot in front of the other as she leaned against the side railing of the porch. BAM! The old wooden railing gave way and she went down to the ground flat on her back. She just laid there not moving. You can see from the photo it wasn't much of a fall to the ground. And it was one of the few places we lived that had grass. We thought blood was coming from the side of her mouth and we all ran down the steps to check on her. It was snuff spit coming out her mouth! (The only time she didn't have a dip of snuff in her mouth was when she was eating.) She peeped out one of her eyes a little, pretending to be knocked out, not realizing she was as obvious as a giant cockroach on rice! One or two of the older sisters were saying, "Mama, you ain't hurt, get up!" while they were pulling on her arms. She moaned and groaned but finally got up. The man was just gone! Don't remember seeing him leave, but he was gone.

Another time Mama and Daddy were fighting like cats and dogs, literally. They were out on the sidewalk in front of the unit and one of 'em had a hammer. Probably Daddy because 1), he was scared of her and 2), had she been the one with the hammer he would've died that day. When Mama was mad enough to fight ya, she had no mercy whatsoever whether she permanently maimed ya or killed ya. Makes no difference to her, she would ram you through with anything she could get her hands on and my sister Judy had that same mentality. They were just a cussing and swinging at one another.

I had run in between them just a crying and a squalling, "Mama, please don't hit Daddy! Daddy, please don't hit Mama!" A car pulled up and it was a cop in an unmarked car. I believe he was a detective, possibly, who just so happened to be driving by and saw the commotion. Had a neighbor actually called the police, a marked police car and a uniformed patrolman would've come. The detective jumped outta his car and ran over to them as fast as he could. He began to yell at both of 'em, "Can't you see this young'un here between ya'll? She could've been killed with that hammer!" He was so mad!!!! Neither one was arrested, though. He finally drove off after they promised to behave. It's amazing how fast they could each calm down once they were faced with the threat of arrest. My crying and begging and risking my life to get them to stop went totally unnoticed by both of 'em. After he left, Mama was just a hollering toward the neighbors, "Which one of ya sons'a bitches called the po-lease?" Of course, no one came out of their home and fessed up.

Although Daddy was sorta scared of Mama, she was also scared of him once he really got mad enough. It took a lot to get him there, but once he was there, he really nutted-up. I guess she figured even though she showed no mercy whatsoever in a fight, once she got him to that same frame of mind, she knew she couldn't win against him. She would always bring up that he was shell-shocked from the war once he was to that point. He would shake and walk in circles with his hands out to each side. He truly acted like his mind had blacked out. After one heated fight and I do mean HEATED fight, he picked up a crow bar and whacked her in the leg right at the knee area.

It was the split end, the part of the crow bar used for pulling nails, which went into her knee. Blood skirted everywhere and we could see pieces of flesh falling out of her knee. We kids were screaming and crying, not knowing what would happen next. The neighbors were so used to hearing the hellraising, fussing, fighting, screaming, crying that they didn't bother to call the police. They had no way of knowing what was going on inside the house and didn't know or give two flips whether someone was being murdered, even if it was us kids being harmed.

At some point Uncle Teat Jordan brought seven of his kids to stay with us. He was actually my daddy's cousin but we called him uncle. He had over a dozen kids and his wife Diane died in childbirth with the last one. Talk about a low life…. He made Mama and Daddy look like good parents. From what I understand, Teat placed four of his youngest kids in an orphanage in Atlanta and sold the last baby to Judge Hardin. What in heck made Mama and Daddy say yes to them moving in with us when they couldn't feed the five they had and half the time our utilities were shut off? I assume they thought in some way they're gonna get money from Teat to drink on or buy food. One of the kids was called "Pig." Her name was Dorothy but her daddy called her Pig. She had something wrong with her and her legs would suddenly give out and she'd fall down. She came across as retarded but some say she wasn't and was actually very smart. I don't know because I never knew her except as a tiny child. I vaguely remember them and don't recall how many boys vs. girls there were. One girl was named Alice, one named Doris, and one named Dorothy are the only names I can remember.

My mama had a glass gallon jar that she made Kool-Aid in when they weren't using it to mix camp heat or Solox. We went into the kitchen and there was Pig standing up in a chair making Kool-Air in that gallon jug. The only reason I remember that is she stuck her entire hand down to the bottom of the jug to stir it up! Over half her arm was down inside that Kool-Aid! We ran out of the kitchen saying, "Eww, Eww, Eww!" I have no idea how long they stayed with us, but I can bet it wasn't long. Mama couldn't stand her own dang kids, let alone someone else's.

As time went on, and the more Mama and daddy got drunk, the longer they stayed drunk. Until they got to where they would tie one on and stay drunk for a month, two months and at times three months. They only sobered up enough to get a hold of another drink. If they could stagger down the street to get a drink, that was as sober as they got. Neither of them had any concern whatsoever as to whether us five kids had anything to eat or what we did or where we wandered off to. Whether or not the house was locked up at night, who came in or who went out.

When they drank like that they would start with liquor or wine. They loved liquor but seldom could afford any of that. Many times, they begin with a half pint or pint of King Cotton wine, which was cheaper than Morgan David if ya can believe that and they graduated downward. Downward to what you might ask? They had almost no money so what little they had, they wanted to make sure they could remain drunk on it for as long as possible. So, they bought rubbing alcohol, which only cost a dime. They watered down the rubbing alcohol just enough to be able to gag it. They did the same with Solox paint thinner and Camp Heat. They could make an entire gallon of "liquor" with a can of Solox paint thinner. The Camp Heat (they called "canned heat") was in small cans used for Sterno cooking, except back then, it was a pink wax type substance, not the liquid version we find in today's Camp Heat. Mama would scrape out all the wax into a dishcloth, twist it around the clump of wax and squeeze and squeeze it until no more pink juice came out, then add water.

Yep, they drank that stuff, and here's the kicker. As with most drunks, they'd pee the bed once they passed out. You haven't experienced such nasal hell until you've walked into a house where two adults who got drunk on paint thinner or Camp Heat laid there and peed and peed all over themselves, (time and time again while wearing the same clothes), and it's soaked into their mattress to mixed with all the other times they peed over the months, and years. Their mattress would collapse with a giant hole in the middle. (Not to even mention us five kids peeing in our bed). Once their mattress had disintegrated to nothing left to lie on, they always managed to find one somewhere that someone was throwing out.

My sister Judy use to say Mama and Daddy were the luckiest da'gum people she ever saw! Just when they HAD to FINALLY put what was left of their mattress on the curb, (which looked just like an enormous cannon had shot a hole through it), low and behold, a neighbor had just placed a mattress, within dragging distance, out on their curb! Dut 'en matter WHY the neighbors had thrown out the mattress or what may be wrong with it or living in it, it still had stuffing and that made it a quality item!

Every single item in our house was always something someone had thrown out. And we lived in poor neighborhoods. We had the furniture and clothes and shoes that other poor people threw away! During our entire time growing up and in everyplace we ever lived, never was a single home furnishing ever bought new. They always managed to get two TV's. One for picture and one for sound, one stacked on top of the other. At times they had to replace a burned-out tube in the back, but they had picture and sound! We always slept on someone's discarded mattresses, cooked in someone's discarded pots and pans, mismatched chipped or cracked dishes, dented canister, our glassware was always mason jars, jelly jars, peanut butter jars, etc.

We had the one lamp that Daddy made from acrylic squares in the VA hospital but it had no shade. Our lights, when the electric was on, was a bare light bulb that hung down from the ceiling in the center of the room with a string hanging from it to turn off and on. I can't remember how old I was the first time I realized what a wall light switch was, but it certainly wasn't at our house. When Daddy would find a box fan on the side of the curb, he'd bring it home to see if it could be fixed. If it was a broken wire, they cut that part out and twisted the wires back together. If it couldn't be fixed because the motor didn't work, they cut off the plug and wire and pitched the fan. That way when he ran across one that had a missing plug or broken wire that couldn't be twisted back together, they were ready.

It's amazing how we never had more than one fan at a time, though. They put it in their room of course, and us being kids, we were too stupid to know we were hot. They would be given or find old quilts, blankets, coats, and that's what we slept on and under in the winter. We never had sheets, just old smelly itchy blankets and quilts and coats. There was a green Army blanket that was wool and itched so bad we didn't know if we were being bit by something or not. Daddy would bring home coats from God knows where, they had a very large box or two in the closet of 'em. Not coats anyone could wear...they'd be men's old gross smelly suit coats, men's long dress coats that probably hasn't been worn by anyone in thirty years or more, weird jackets, heavy wool coats. But in the wintertime, that's what we piled on top of us in bed to keep warm.

At times we could barely turn over from the weight of all those coats. But it kept us warm and didn't smell any worse than our mattresses already did. I cringe to think where they got our bed pillows; I just know it wasn't from a store. Our washcloths were torn up rags, our dishcloths were larger torn up rags. Flour sacks came with tiny blue, pink, or yellow flowers printed on them and became either more dishrags, or underwear without elastic. Hand sewn in the shape of panties, but I had to hold them up by hand when I walked. If I could find a safety pin to hold 'em up, I could go outside and run and play without my drawers falling down around my ankles! There were five of us, so I only got one pair drawers at a time. And I'd pee in 'em every single night! With a family of seven, we were probably known as the Peein' Palmer's behind our backs. Hard to believe even roaches and rats would want to come in our house.

Another place to score some rags, towels, or underwear is checking washers at the Laundromat. If something was missed by the last user that was exciting! Pay dirt! On at least one occasion a sister stole some towels out of a dryer at the Laundromat. I don't remember which sister, just the excitement of getting towels!!! I remember year's later hearing folks who lived in the project complaining that their clothes, sheets, or blankets were stolen from their clothesline. Most everyone in the project had a washing machine in their kitchen but there was no place for a dryer, so just about every yard had clotheslines.

The ones who had no washing machine, washed their clothes in the bathtub on a scrub board, then hung them on the clothesline. So, I wouldn't doubt if Mama and or daddy helped themselves to a few things while living there. I do know sometime later, one of my sisters, who shall remain nameless, would go to the project and steal clothes from the clotheslines. She also stole from the stores downtown, but heck, I can't fault her too much. Mama and daddy sure didn't buy us anything, so it was up to us to get clothes and shoes, coats, etc., from wherever we could.

Uncle Red, a thin elderly man who was sweeter than honey and always had money bought Jewel and Judy each a Pea coat, a pair of white marching boots with tassels and a baton. How I envied them. But I did sneak and wear the boots and twirl the baton when they weren't looking. Uncle Red was no kin really; he was a life-long friend of my granny's and her husband Carl. Kids did not call adults by their first name back then; they were either addressed as Mr. or Uncle.

He didn't have a family of his own to buy for and he also bought things for Aunt Shirley and Emmie. He obviously loved to shower kids with gifts, although he didn't seem to notice Dale, Joyce, or I existed. I heard years later he was found dead in a field behind the boys' club. He was not one of my mama's boyfriends and I never heard of him trying to take advantage of a child. He was just a sweet old soul doing what he could do to make a child happy.

Mama and Daddy managed to get drunk even without a penny to their name. Seems there was always a "friend" stopping by who could afford a bottle of rubbing alcohol and more than willing to hang around and get drunk with them. My daddy would go to relatives' homes and sneak their aftershave or cologne or mouthwash or vanilla extract. I've seen him gag so many times trying to keep mouthwash down. The devil had such a strong hold on them; it was no longer a choice for them to drink but a necessity to live!

Mama occasionally would have a couple dimes, a nickel, and a couple pennies or some small amount of change. She would stack it and tie it up in the corner of a lady's hankie. It was tied so tight, you could break three fingernails trying to untie it. (Daddy had bought Mama a box of three white cotton hankies for their anniversary or her birthday some time before down at one of the 5 and 10 cents store, maybe Woolworth's. They each had an embroidered flower in one corner, one in pink, one purple and one yellow and probably cost less than a dollar.) She would put that hankie with her treasured and highly guarded 27 cents in her bra, and many times she'd tie the other end of the hanky to her bra strap! Made no difference how hungry we were, how long we had been without food, she would fight us over that 27 cents!

She was super strong compared to us and she'd kill ya if you tried to get it from her. Of course, once she had totally passed out drunk, we could get the change from her, but we learned pretty dang quick not to "roll her" like we did Daddy. We could roll him if he was really, really dog drunk and passed out to the world and he wasn't lying on top of the one hip pocket he had some change in. Even when we found he had a little money and we took it, he never mentioned it when he woke up even if it was close to a dollar's worth of change, where Mama would kill ya if she woke up and realized her 27 cents was missing. I don't remember ever rolling Daddy and him having any folding money; it was always just a little change.

While living on Pearl Ave I remember one time

Joyce and I found some mustard or it may have been mayonnaise in the kitchen, but for argument's sake, I'll just say mustard because I'm not sure which one it was now but it doesn't matter, we'd eat either of them. When I say we had nothing to eat at home, I literally mean NOTHING! If we could find a little flour, we'd mix it with water and fry it. Even if we had no margarine or grease to fry it in, we cooked it and ate it. We called it Pone-Pone bread although it certainly wasn't.

If we found some can milk in the fridge, we drank it. If there was any of that thick dark Karo syrup we drank it, or even table sugar, we'd eat it. There was absolutely nothing else to eat and it was just a small amount of mustard in the bottom of a round glass jar. So, we decided if we could "borrow" four slices of bread from a neighbor we could make us each a mustard sandwich! After a whole lot'a going back in forth as to which one of us was gonna have the nerve to go ask someone for the bread, we decided to both go but Joyce would do the asking. "Now remember to ask for FOUR pieces of bread," I told her. So, we went a couple doors down and knocked on this elderly lady's door. We had never actually met her, or spoken with her, and certainly didn't know her name but I'm sure she was very aware of who we were. Most likely she had peered out her window many times and watched the Palmer Drama.

She finally came to the door and opened it only slightly and asked us what we wanted. She sorta reminded me of how Mama Hall may ask a couple kids at her door what the Sam Hill they want. Joyce very politely asked if we could "borrow" four slices of bread from her. (I'm sure she knew fat chance we'd ever have some extra bread to pay her back!) She glared at us for a moment then said, "Wait," closed the door and came back after a while with four heels, you know, the end slices. It took her long enough that we wondered if 'en she snuck out the back door! Now back then there were no twister seals on bread. Each end on a loaf of bread had a sticker, like a 3-inch or maybe 4-inch square with the name brand printed on it and that's what sealed it close.

Once opened, you had to sorta fold the wrapper under or place it into a container or something, but there was no replacing that sticker. So obviously, the lady opened a new loaf to get the other two heel slices. She gave us a look of disgust and closed the door without saying a word. Here are two little young'uns, ages three and five, or four and six at the most, standing there, very underweight, skin and bone practically, whose parents are known all over the neighborhood, all over town really, for laying drunk and yet someone can bring themselves to make the kids feel like a nuisance for asking for some bread. It wasn't like we asked for a bowl of hot buttered grits to go with it or anything. We were so embarrassed! You might not think at such a young age we would've even noticed her disdain for us, but we did notice, and it hurt our feelings so much that we never asked another neighbor for food. Even when we went to our aunt's homes or our granny's, we never "asked" for food, no matter how hungry we were. We'd always wait to be offered something to eat. But looking back, maybe that old lady was struggling already and just barely getting by and here comes kids from the most hated family in the neighborhood wanting to "borrow" bread.

But as the years went by, we found that very same treatment toward us Palmer girls, everywhere we went practically, especially from neighbors, schoolteachers, and classmates.

While living there on Pearl Ave, we five girls were taken away by the authorities and placed in a Children's Home. It very well may have been the episode where Mama and Daddy were fighting out on the sidewalk and daddy holding a hammer that got us taken away. I cannot remember why we were taken. It also may have been that Jewel, Judy and Dale weren't in school regularly. Joyce and I weren't in school yet.

They took us to Old Lady Cooper's home. She was mean as a snake and twice as ugly. She may have asked if we wet the bed since she has had many, many kids in her home over the years and knew that was a possibility, or someone told her we did, or we had a strong urine odor, (my bet). I don't recall which one of us gave her an answer or what the answer was.

There were other kids there, but I don't remember how many or how old they might have been at that time. I remember seeing Old Lady Cooper sitting in a big chair in the living room cutting her toenails over a towel or small blanket with large scissors, which she used the point of them to clean out from under her toenails. When she had finished, she took all four corners of the towel or blanket toward the center and holding it all together she had one of the kids step outside and shake the toenails off it. A short time later someone knocked on the front door and she sent a kid to answer it.

A little girl stepped in holding a brown paper grocery bag. She said, "Miss Cooper, here's all the fruit and nuts to make the fruitcake. Mama said let her know if you need anything else and there's no rush." I no doubt would've never remembered that conversation had we not watched the Cooper Hag take those same scissors, without washing them or her hands and began to cut up the fruit for that lady's fruitcake. As gross as our standard of living was, and as young as we were, we couldn't even fathom someone doing that! It left a gagging impression forever in my mind.

Later that night as we were being put to bed, Old Lady Cooper informed us in no uncertain terms and as a matter-of-fact as she could, IF we happen to pee in one of her beds, she will cut our heads off. I don't know what my older sisters thought about that but me and

Joyce believed her. We were so scared we'd pee during the night; I prayed, and I'm sure she did as well, for God to let us not pee the bed. We even tried to stay awake all night but eventually fell asleep. When we woke up and realized we had indeed wet the bed, we hid under the bed hoping she couldn't find us.

We were trembling and crying and just knew she was gonna cut our heads off. But Jewel, Judy and Dale had other plans, (probably because they had wet the bed also!) They grabbed us up and the five of us took off out the backdoor and over the fence, we all held hands and ran up the alley toward home. Joyce's feet never touched the ground; she just bent her knees and went along for the ride. (What's funny, Joyce's future husband, Ricky Crawford, was a little boy playing in his backyard and watched us all run away).

Once we got home, low and behold, Mama was sober! Probably because she was mad as a hornet that someone had the guts to take "HER" kids away and she was getting ready to show them the wrath of Lorraine!!! Mama knew they'd be looking for us so she put us in a closet and dumped a box of clothes and old blankets over us. Sure, enough the cops showed up. Our cousin Ivy Walters had stopped by and they were gonna take him thinking he was one of the Palmer kids. He was saying, "I ain't going nowhere!" Mama was saying, "That's my nephew, my sister's boy and ya ain't seen no hell till Mae finds out ya took her boy!"

They decided to believe her, I reckon, because they left, and we crawled out from under the heap of coats and blankets from the closet and they never came back. I guess we weren't worth the trouble.

One of the few cautions I ever remember being told by Mama was, "Never touch a moving train or it'll suck you under it!" Well low and behold there just happened to be some train tracks in front of our house. We had to cross the street, walk a little ways to a set of wooden steps, go over the wooden bridge and down another set of wooden steps, which landed right dab beside the railroad tracks. Jewel said she didn't believe it would suck us under the train and the very next time we heard a train coming, we took off to the bridge.

We got to the train and stood there running our hands across the freight cars. Jewel said, "See there! I knew it wouldn't suck us under!" (In Mama's defense, the train was moving really slow so maybe it has to be moving fast.) So, we all moseyed back to the house to inform Mama she was wrong about that. Or in Jewel's words, "You lied, old woman. I got as close to that train as I could get and it didn't suck me under!" Mama looked at us as if she had no clue what we were talking about.

We were out playing jump rope one day when a soldier walked by. There were only two of us, either Dale and I or Joyce and I and we had the rope tied to something on the other end. It made it hard to jump the

rope because the tied end wasn't turning like a person would turn it. So, we asked him to turn that end for us. He did until we got tired of jumping rope. He said his name was Jim Ryan or Rhine, and we took him home. We introduced him to Mama, left him sitting there with her and ran back out to play. "What were we thinking?" Ya don't take a man home to Mama! Who knew?

Dale came home with a dog one day, said it followed her home. It was some sort of a medium size dog with blotchy colors of brown, orange, and black. Looked about like this.

Someone named her Brownie, probably Dale. She was mostly an outside dog because Mama didn't allow animals in our house. And, of course, Mama had a fit about a dog and said Dale can't keep her but the dog wouldn't leave and finally Mama stopped griping about it. She even started taking a liking to Brownie and actually fed her! Go figure! Well, daddy shows up with a parakeet that one of his fares gave him while driving a cab. They gave him the cage and everything in it also. It was a pretty powder blue parakeet that daddy named Pete and he put the cage and bird in the living room.

Well, Brownie got herself pregnant somewhere out there unbeknownst to any of us. It was getting on in the winter and really, really cold outside, so daddy brought home a 'banana' box that was long and narrow. He thought it would be okay to let Brownie sleep in that box at night since it was so cold out. Of course, Mama raised hell, but he said it would just be at night. There was a white open bookshelf against the wall, looked homemade. Daddy sat the box under the bottom shelf hoping Mama wouldn't have too much of a problem with the dog staying in at night. Brownie had about seven puppies and they were all in that banana box. Someone left the bird cage open and we found the birds blue feathers in that banana box with Brownie and the puppies. No sign of the bird, just its feathers. The pups didn't even have their eyes open yet so we knew it had to be Brownie that ate that poor bird. As soon as those pups were weaned, they got rid of 'em somehow.

Chapter 5

We moved from Pearl Ave to Welsh Lane which was and still is a dirt alley behind Broad Street. And Brownie moved there too. It was a doubled sided shotgun house, a duplex. We moved into the left side, just the three rooms once again for a family of seven. The rent was cheaper there than Pearl Ave. Probably $10 to $15 a month or so.

This is the actual house, 1718 Welsh Lane. We lived on the left side and a family of nine lived on the right side. Below is a picture of what it closely resembled

back then. It was not painted, had no awnings, and the porch was all wood, no slats, just a top rail and one could crawl under the house by going under the front porch or on the sides. There was no ramp, no gate, and no beautiful shrubbery as you see here. Looks like some uppity folks done moved in! They even have a window air conditioner in the window I see.

This is exactly what the house looked like on Welsh Lane other than the roof line and a two by four banister going between those four-by-four support posts on the porch. A single two by four from the center support post to the wall divided the porch into two. Inside wasn't much different than the outside, unpainted lath, and plaster walls. Lath is narrow horizontal boards. The floors were unpainted wood as well as the ceilings. Dale's dog Brownie could get under the house, she was never allowed inside again, no matter how cold it got in the winter. Brownie was on her on as to what she ate. It was a very rare occasion for her to have a can of dog food; she probably ate rats, birds and figs that fell from the tree.

Once we played a mean joke on an elderly black lady. Right at dusk but not all the way dark she'd turned the corner from Frank Street onto Welsh Lane and walked past our house and on up the alley she'd turned left behind the church up there. I guess she was heading home from working some place because every day she came by. We had come across a lady's

nylon stocking that we filled with the powdery sand from the alley. We shaped it just like a leg and tied off the open end with a long string. After laying the "leg" in the middle of the alley, we laid on our bellies under the porch while holding on to the other end of the string. Here she comes… ya could barely see the leg till ya was right up on it. As she got close to it, we began to pull the string so the leg looked as if it was moving. She screamed and ran around it and went hollering all the way up the alley. We laughed and laughed…. Later we tried to pull the same joke on a man coming up the alley. He got almost to it and it began to move and he just stopped. He placed his hands just above his knees and lean down looking under our porch. He said, "Wut'a you kids doin' under there? Tryin' to pull someone's leg?" Then HE laughed and laughed as he walked on.

Here is my feeble attempt to describe the inside of a shotgun home. These houses came with a kitchen sink attached to the wall, no cabinet underneath, just a sink with bare pipes exposed. That's how ya knew it was the kitchen! The bathroom consisted of a claw footed tub and toilet only and it was always dark in there because there was no light fixture or window. We used the fireplace for heat for quite a while but of course most of the heat went up the chimney and it had to be constantly stirred and messed with to keep it going. Don't have a clue where they finally scored a potbelly stove, but eventually one sat in front of the fireplace. It had a pipe coming from the top rear that connected to the wall above the mantle.

No way could we afford to burn wood so we burned coal. It was the heat for the entire house and served to heat water also. Seldom did we have the natural gas turned on so to have hot water we sat a pot or pots on the potbelly stove. That's how we washed dishes and heat bath water. Wherever we lived the heat source was always the closest to Mama and her bed just as the fan was in the summer. When they were sober, and we had coal, she would fire up that potbelly stove till it was red hot. Mama was very cold-natured and Daddy was very hot-natured. He would have to open the front door and leave it standing wide open to stand the heat, even though it might be in the 20s or 30s outside. It was the start of WWIII every single time he did that. She cussed him for everything under the sun and he would tell her to stop beating her chops.

On more than one occasion late at night we'd hear daddy trying to wake Mama saying, "Lorraine, Lorraine, there's somebody out there messing around the house. Sounds like they're trying to get in the backdoor or trying to open a window. You hear it? Lorraine, Lorraine, somebody's out there, I tell ya I've been hearing it!" She'd get up, casually get a hammer or a crowbar or something and go out the front door. She would walk between the houses, leaning down to see if she could see anyone under the house, walk to the backyard which was fenced in and very dark.

She'd look all back there and the back porch, come back to the front and come in saying, "There ain't no damn body out there, Ed!" We thought it was funny that he was too scared to go check outside in the dark but she wasn't. There weren't any street lights in that ally, no porch lights either, so it would've been hard to see someone hiding out there and especially under the house. But she was just the type to dare a prowler to come out from under the house and face the Grim REAPER, AKA—Lorraine.

We use to sit in the fig tree that was right off the back porch and eat those figs as fast as they ripened. We could always tell when there were ripe figs ready to eat because wasps were all over the tree. When the figs were still green, ya could pick one and the "milk" that came from the stem was sticky and made perfect glue. Just about as good as Elmer's!

There was a white cinder block building across the alley from our house, slightly diagonally to our left if you were looking out the front door. One day in the middle of the afternoon, Judy was laying on that white wicker sofa in the front room. The front door was standing open and she laid there just starring out for the longest time. Suddenly she starts screaming these blood curdling screams! I mean screaming and shaking and crying all at one time. We all came a running to see what the heck was wrong. She kept saying there were skeletons up on top of that white building and they were moving around and talking. No one could see anything but her and she was very emphatic they were there, and they were watching her too. Mama told her there was nothing up there and if she didn't shut that screaming up, she'd give her something to scream about. Either she was having a daymare while wide awake, or she seen something! A daymare is being caught up in a thought-created reality and not knowing it.

A family named Masters lived in the same structure as we did but on the right side. We shared a porch with them except for that single wooden banister dividing us. They had six kids and Mr. Masters mother living with them in their shotgun house. Besides the parents, Allen and Marie, and his mother, there was Pat, George, David, Mary, Debra, and Janet, if I remember correctly. In the beginning we didn't get along with them because every time that little Janet came out on the porch and saw me or Joyce, she would place her two boney fingers over her lips and spit on us! She was about three years old and we never seen her or the four-year-old, Debra, wearing clothes.

They both only wore what looked like use to be white panties. They were like the toddlers' cotton training panties but they were so stretched out and filthy and the crotch hung down to their knees or more. Their bellies had dirty sticky black smudges all over them; their hair was matted, and their feet were so dirty they were plum black. Janet would lean forward on that one dirty foot with her drawers hanging down to her knees and SPIT! The memory of that makes me laugh out loud now but not so much when it was happening! We couldn't believe how mean they were! Finally, we told Mama because we knew she'd nut up on 'em. AND she did! Mama went flying out that door and hollering for their mother Marie to get her ass out there. When Marie came out on the porch, Mama told her, "If any of yo young'uns spits on my young'uns again, I'm gonna whoop yo ass!" Mama couldn't stand the thoughts of someone spitting on someone period! Plus, she loved a good fight! It was so funny; she always called Marie, Mare-ree. We all did because we thought that was her name since that's what Mama called her. Heck, I was in my thirty's when I heard someone call the name MARIE on TV and suddenly it hit me, *Hey, I bet that was my neighbors name back in Welsh's Lane, not Mare-ree but Marie!* I laughed till my sides hurt at how dumb we were!

The entire Masters family had head lice and of course we Palmers got them too. (But in their defense, it was common back then when you had kids in school. It was very easy to catch head-lice and very hard to get rid of, especially with a family of nine in a three room house). We all got bed bugs as well.CHINSES as Mama called them. Their grandmother who lived there with them use to sit on the porch with newspapers across her lap and lean over it to comb her hair. She would have a ton of head lice piled on the papers! I couldn't believe all that was in her hair! Mama washed our heads in kerosene and took all the mattresses outside and the white wicker sofa and literally sprayed them all down with kerosene. Lawd, we had to smell that smell for nights on end! But she got rid of all the head lice and bed bugs! She borrowed a hosepipe and hosed down the inside floors and walls and swept the water out with a broom. She was highly creative like that.

But eventually we all began to get along with the Masters and we liked them. We played with their kids and had lots of fun with them. Joyce and I especially loved having six more kids to play with. We played Hide n Seek, 1-10 Red Light, Red Rover Red Rover, and Hopscotch with them. Kinda hard to play those games when it was just two of us. Mama never did like them, but she never liked anyone that I know of and we liked everyone unless they gave us a reason not to.

Once Allen's brother, (I think it was his brother) was running from the cops and he ran up on the Masters side of the porch, I guess hoping his brother was home and his brother would protect him. He made it all the way to the porch where the cops grabbed him and they began to beat him with night sticks unmercifully! We could hear his skull crack with every blow. I remember getting very nauseous seeing the blood and hearing those sounds. We all cried and begged the police to stop. They said he had molested a child somewhere. Even though he had it coming it was pitiful.

The oldest Masters daughter, Patricia, even got me a job selling newspapers on the corner of Reynolds and Broad Street's, (a very good corner) I might add. I look back now at how dumb I was, even dumb for a kid, and I laugh so hard at myself. The newspapers were a dime each and it was during Master's Golf week. An Augusta Chronicle truck came by, gave us each several stacks of newspapers tied with some jute. They also provided a coin changer for each of us to wear. So here I am selling newspapers and every time someone would stop at the intersection and stick their dime out for a paper, as I handed them their paper I'd say, "Which one are you for, the Masters or the Palmers?"

They would give me a strange look and shake their head and drive away. I thought to myself, dang these out of towners are unfriendly! They must be some of them damn Yankee's daddy says he runs across while driving a cab! I wanted to know who they were rooting for because Pat was a Masters and I was a Palmer! Of course, years later I realize the golfers ARE the MASTERS and Arnold Palmer is a single person, not a whole team! LOL! Anyway, after selling a bunch of papers I was getting tired, not to mention sick and tired of those hoity-toity damn Yankee's attitude toward me, and having a lot of change in my coin changer, I left the rest of the papers sitting there in a stack right there on the curb and ran over to a little store on the corner. I had enough dimes, nickels, and quarters to buy snack cakes, candy, RCs, whatever I wanted! YAY! I was happier than a hog in warm mud! After buying a bag of stuff, I moseyed on home and didn't give it another thought. Until years later, (probably about the same time I realized Pat's mama's name was NOT pronounced Mare-ree), but it dawned on me, *hey, the* Augusta Chronicle *probably expected me to turn in that money and the coin changer! LOL!!!!!!!!!!!* I don't know what I ever did with the coin changer. Most likely, it just became one of my toys.

While I still had some newspaper money left, at some point, Joyce and I walked a few alleys over where there was a little store that had a juke box. We chose a song to play so we could dance! We thought we looked so cool doing our version of the jitterbug. We even threw our arms across one another's shoulder and slid them across and down each other's arm until our hands met again while never missing a beat with our feet! We were dancing and stomping so hard, why if he hadn't had cement floors we would've knocked the jars of pickled pig's feet plum off the shelves! After just one dance, the clerk said, "There is no dancing allowed in here." But he did watch us dance that first dance till the end before he said anything.

He probably thought we were cuter than a bug's ear dancing just like we thought we were auditioning for American Bandstand, even though we were only six and eight years old. Or maybe we were probably stinking up the place! We seldom had a bath, we peed the bed every single night, and we slept in our clothes which seldom got washed! But as we left, we mumbled to one another why does he have a jukebox then if 'en ya cain't dance! Who the heck's gonna come into his store and play the jukebox while buying a loaf of bread and a can of Pork and Beans? Oh well, we didn't go back to his store.

Welsh Lane dead ended into Frank St, another alley and a woman named Donna Johnson lived in the house on Frank Street that faced Welsh lane. If we stood in our alley and looked that way, we would be looking directly at her house. Well, there was a man that stood out in front of her place all the time facing our alley. He was there more often than not and we didn't have a clue who he was or why he seemed to always be standing there. But Joyce would run up to him and ask him for a dime every so often. He usually gave her one and then she'd say, "Can I have one for my sista too?" He'd give her another one. If he told her he didn't have a dime, she'd ask for a cigarette. He'd give her one and of course she needed another one for her sista! LOL, I was always too shy to be the one asking, but there wasn't a shy bone in Joyce's body.

Not sure what we did with the cigarettes he gave us, neither of us smoked… yet. Maybe we wanted them for bartering, who knows? Sometimes he only gave us a nickel and there was a store in the alley directly behind our house inside another house. The old white man who owned it was bedridden and laid there in his bed overlooking the store part. He had a young black man named Jesse running the store for him. Jesse had an identical twin named Willie and we never knew which one was working at any given time, so we called them both Jesse. They sold penny candy from a glass case and cookies from the clear plastic Murray tins and colas mostly.

We thought nothing of asking for two Mary Jane's, two Squirrel Nuts, and a nigga baby. They were little tiny chocolate babies and everyone called them Nigga Babies. He was kind enough to never react to that, but we actually thought that's what they were named from the manufacturers. We were so dumb! I so wish I could apologize to him now. The country was a differ-

ent world back in the 1950s, especially in the South. We didn't even realize the "N" word was a bad word back then.

We (Joyce and I) roamed the streets all day, seldom stayed home. Mama never knew or cared where we were or what we were up to. We walked the canal bank and a few times and even sat at the water's edge and put out feet in the brown cloudy water to cool off. You couldn't see through the water at all. We were never told to look out for water moccasins or gators, not to mention any other kind of snakes that could be hidden in the grass. We could spot a house a mile away that someone had recently vacated but new tenants haven't moved into yet. They were always unlocked and we'd go in and look around for anything we could fine. Back then those who had a telephone and moved, it was the practice of the telephone company to have them leave the phone behind and it was always still in service. The new tenants I assume would get that same phone number if they wanted phone service. Usually that was the only thing left behind in an otherwise empty house.

So. me and Joyce would sit in the floor and commence to dialing! We never had a phone in our home and just loved making phone calls! We didn't have a clue who we were calling, just dialed some random number and then ask anyone who answered if their refrigerator was running. Sometimes the person we called would cuss us out, accusing us of being unsupervised stupid children! LOL… they had no idea how right on they were! If they were particularly nasty toward us and IF we could remember the number we just dialed, we'd call 'em back a couple times to really get on their nerves. But since we didn't know any pranks other than that one, we soon tired of the phone and moved on.

Most folks then had what they called a party line so they shared the connection with one to two other folks. Each home just had a different ring, two short, or one long, or two long rings so they'd know which home was receiving a call. Sometimes we'd luck out and we'd hear a conversation already on the line. We'd listen and if we became bored with what they were saying, we'd interject some words here and there, like, "Really?" or "Is that so?" We'd hear whoever we were interrupting say, "Wut?" "Wut'd ya say?" The other person would say, "Wut?" Then silence, then they'd resume their conversation and we'd do it again. Finally, one of 'em would say something like, "Ya brats bet'a be gittin' off this phone 'fore I call the po-lease!" We'd laugh and laugh. Ahh, good times!

Once we walked to the other end of Welsh Lane but instead of turning right onto Crawford Ave and heading over to Chaffee Park, we crossed over Crawford Ave and continued up Welsh Lane on the other side. We came to the back of the Ezekiel Harris House and it was empty. I can still remember that old musty smell there and thinking it seemed even older that the one we lived in on Welsh Lane which was built in the 1800s! Dale and Judy were with us that time and it was probably their idea to go in that house. I can't speak for them but I did not recognize the house from the back, even though I would've known from Broad Street we were entering the "White House" as we use to call it.

This was before we ever knew it was supposedly haunted or that Mama and Daddy once lived there, at least I didn't know. We walked up onto the back porch and upstairs and then up another staircase that went into the attic, and we had never seen an attic before. One of us yelled, "Hey yaw, look, there's two stairs! Must've been rich people living here!" We thought that was so neat! We looked out the window in the attic, I should say barely looked out the window since it appeared the glass had never been cleaned, and we were excited that we were so high up!!! (Lawd, Lawd, anything or anyone could have been in that house!).

There was an old trunk sitting under the window, the only thing in the entire attic that I remember. We opened it up and there was a tray with compartments that had lids over them. We lifted the lids and there were confederate bills in them! Lots of them! We removed the tray and there was a light green evening gown in the bottom of the trunk. It was strapless, sweetheart bust line with lime green tulle overlay from the waist down to the floor. The tulle was faded and all crinkly; it looked and smelled very old. We grabbed the gown and the confederate money and made a bee-line home. Mama said the money was worthless and she threw it out. We played in the gown, pretending to be somebody rich and elegant. (Not realizing someone rich and elegant did indeed once own it).

Mama eventually came across it when she was on the warpath and put her foot on it and proceeded to rip it to shreds. She always looked for something to destroy when she was mad which pretty much every day when she was sober. She usually destroyed what meant the most to Daddy or one of us kids and since we had so much fun playing in the gown its days were numbered from the moment we brought it home. That's our fault! We should've had enough sense to at least pretend the gown made our lives a living hell, it would've lasted forever. But it's sad now that the house is a museum and those were most likely belongings of the original owners. They would be highly valued now and I wish we had left them alone. I really hate being classified as a dumb hick, but there are times looking back, I'm amazed how dumb and utterly stupid we were... all of us!

We crawled into the basement window of a church and 'visited' the classrooms. We drew on the blackboards with their pretty colored chalk and drank and ate any snacks we found. They had an easel covered in felt and had colored cut-outs of Jesus and the disciples, trees, rocks, buildings, etc. We played with those while telling our unlearned version of biblical stories to a make-believe audience. "Now here you see Jesus walked up dirt roads just like ours and even though he was wearing sandals, his feet never got dirty, cause he was Jesus see." "Mary also had a little lamb," and "Here is where Jesus turned water into wine and Mama and Daddy wished He had turned ALL the water into WINE!"

Joyce and I visited the city dump on a regular basis. I couldn't even tell you where that was located now or how far we walked to get to it. But we always found "good" stuff. Really good stuff! We mostly wanted something to eat and the local bakery regularly threw out outdated baked goods that were individually wrapped. Our favorite was the Honey Buns and we ate them on the spot with our unwashed hands after digging through mounds and mounds of garbage to find them. We were generally barefooted and we stepped on all sorts of stuff climbing those huge mounds of garbage. Our feet would sink down till half our legs were buried and it was hard to ma-neuver, but luckily, we could pull our legs back out of the heaps. There were animal carcasses, slop, broken glass, and sharp metal pieces along with medical supplies all mixed in together. Mound after mound of that stuff, stunk to high heaven! We found a bicycle wheel that had a flat tire.

We searched and searched for the rest of that bicycle and couldn't find it. We wondered why in the world someone would keep the rest of the bicycle with only one wheel so we figured the rest of it had to be there somewhere but we never found it. We gathered up old baby dolls and used hypodermic needles. There were vials of medicines in tiny glass bottles with a flat rubber top. I suppose the hospitals threw them out due to them being expired or some such. (I bet they wouldn't do that these days.) We took a bunch of the medicine vials home too and every day we played with that stuff, giving the dolls shots. We had the dolls all lined up and filled the hypodermics with the medicines, then inserted them in the dolls heads or the butts and gave them all shot after shot. (It's a wonder if they didn't come to life!)

We broke off many of the needles attempting to stick them in the dolls butts which were made of a much harder plastic than the heads. Mama could plainly see what we were playing with and never once said one word about it. Never asked where we got those things or where we had been or any warning of what a used needle may be infected with. She was real motherly like that, just as long as we didn't bother her. We also gave the dolls haircuts and drew new faces on them with ink pens. They may have been uglier but they sure weren't boring anymore.

There was hardly a day went by that Joyce and I didn't tour Augusta. We especially loved going to Sears and Roebucks on Walton Way. It was always so nice and cool inside and they had water fountains with ice cold water to drink. We rode those escalators up, then down, then up, then down. We'd go to the bathroom and back to the water fountain, back to the escalators. It never, ever, ever occurred to us to steal something though. I was shocked to find out some of the other sisters did steal. I'm not faulting them though, we had nothing and that was the only way to get anything.

Actually, I'm shocked it never occurred to Joyce or me to steal, seeing all those pretty clothes in Sears, but we didn't. There was a school nearby over that way. I don't know the name of it because we went to John Milledge. But we went inside that school one day and there in the hallway was a square table, I reckon it was a card table and it had lunch trays lined up across it. The trays were lined with napkins and on the napkins were little sugar cubes with a pretty pink dot on top of each one. We said, "Wow, they never served us candy like this at John Milledge!" We grabbed a whole hand full each and took off. (I guess that WAS stealing!)

But we justified that theft because we somehow knew that candy was free to the students. But we ate a lot of those, as many as we could fit into our hand and run with. Only to discover years later, those were polio vaccines. Once again, Merciful Lord Jesus looking out for us. We never knew back then that Mama's brother, Uncle

Raymond, was the manager of Kelly's Hamburger and it was just up the street. Had we known, we would've gone in there to see if he would volunteer us some french fries or something. Shucks, missed out on that.

Somebody told us there was a lady who had a water head baby up on one of those streets off of Hicks Street. We wanted to see that! So, we took off over there! We walked up on her porch, knocked on her door, and when she answered it, we just blurted out so matter-of-factly, "We come to see your water head baby." She stood there kinda stunned for a moment. I said, "We heard you had one." She slammed that door in our face!!! She never even said whether or not she had one, let alone let us see it. We walked away murmuring something to one another like, "Maybe it's asleep and she's afraid we'll wake it up" and "Yeah, or maybe she don't even have a water head baby!"

Either way, we decided SHE was rude! At times we passed a house that had an upper porch and a lower porch. Hanging from the bottom of the upper porch they had four or five coconuts with faces painted on them. We had never seen a coconut before and we thought they were some sort of heads from something. Didn't look quiet human but more demonic than anything. As we walked past that house, we always tried to walk faster. Joyce would always say, "They're so smooky!" (She meant spooky) and I'd say, "I know, don't look at 'em, Joyce."

On one of our outings, we passed a really nice house where there was a brother and a sister out front kicking a ball around. It rolled toward Joyce and I and one of us gently kicked it back toward them. They both were much older and taller than us, but they were very friendly and began talking to us. Asking where we lived and such. It was hot outside and the girl asked if we would like to have an ice cream cone. Of course, our eyes lit up like searchlights and we both said YEAH! She led us around to their backyard and up on their back porch. Low and behold, they had a box of cones hanging on their wall and a deep freezer right on the porch! She opened up that deep freezer and there were those same types of barrels of ice cream just like at the Lakeview Drugstore! All kinds of flavors too! They even had an ice cream scoop just like the drug-store uses that rolls the ice cream into a ball.

We had no idea you could have cones and ice cream scoopers and such at your house! We were just mes-merized by their house, their generosity, their friendli-ness, and their ice cream cones! I believe we both chose chocolate and she put two great big scoops on each one. We walked around their backyard while we ate them, or devoured them I should say. We thought we had some new friends and we could go over there sometimes and get an ice cream. But there was some-thing off there. She and her brother were standing side by side watching us and although they were facing in our direction, their eyes would go to one side toward one another while they mumbled something. It was sorta eerie the way they began acting and just the way they looked at us, and when I think back on it, it gives me the creeps.

I believe it was God's protection once again that we never went back there. I mean we have been looked at, glared at, made fun of, ostracized, and made to feel like poor white trash enough times that we knew it wasn't that and there was something different about this situation. But for whatever reason, we never went back there and for two little kids not to ever go back where they were given free ice cream, I find that strange.

Daddy drove a cab then and if he had some tip money or if it was payday, he liked to stop off at a bar called Frank and Broad. Actually, it was called Frank and Broad because it was a bar at the corner of Frank and Broad streets. (Wow, the things we realize later in life!) They had a jukebox, a pool table and a bar the men sat lined up to drink and that he did! We lived just around the corner and two houses up from there and he would come from around the corner staggering home many, many times. We knew if Mama was sober, all hell was about to break loose and then she's gonna tie one on too. And for the next month or two they would lay drunk and he would be fired from his job.

I remember once being so hungry, Mama was drunk and we hadn't eaten in a couple days and he'd been out getting more to drink. He was coming up those side steps to the porch and I was on the porch. I stopped him and ask if I could have a quarter or a dime to get something to eat. He said, as only he could say in a raised voice, "Uh-uh, Uh-uh, I ain't got no money." I grabbed the cigarettes from his shirt pocket and said, "Okay, I'll eat these, then!" I began to break a cigarette up and put it in my mouth and started chewing it.

He walked on past me and into the house as if to say, "Carry on, who cares." He did not care that we were hungry, that he had no clue when we had eaten last, and that there was nothing in the house to eat. When I say there was nothing in the house to eat, I mean there was zilch, zero, nada, nothing, absolutely NOTHING to eat. I spat out the cigarette, which made me sick and if I had had something in my stomach to throw up, it would've come up.

So many times we went looking for Daddy hoping he would buy us something to eat. Mama passed out at home, we'd walk over to the bar at the corner of Frank and Broad. We would peer through the glass door on the side toward the back and sure enough, he'd be sitting there at the bar drinking. We'd go inside to ask him for a little money, back then a quarter was the most we could ever hope for, usually got a dime or a nickel if anything. He almost always said he didn't have any. But he frequently pumped nickel after nickel in that jukebox. He'd play that song he loved that had just come out, "North to Alaska." Plus, he loved "The Ballad of Thunder Road" by Robert Mitchum and "White Lighting" One way or the other he was gonna hear North to Alaska. The bartender would get upset with little kids being in the bar begging him for some change and he would tell Daddy he had to leave. But he still almost never volunteered a single dime.

So, we'd wait till he laid down and passed out and we ever so slowly began to pull on the lining of his hip pocket. His pants were usually navy blue and the lining was white so it was easy to see even in the semi dark. There are so many times we'd get the lining almost out to where we could get to the change and his hand would fly down to his pocket like greased lightning! He would put his giant hand inside his pocket and go back to sleep. Sometimes he would say, "Uh-Uh, Uh-Uh" while shoving the lining back inside his pocket and keep his hand inside so we couldn't get to his change. Never once looking up at us, or caring that we were hungry. But generally, he tried to remember to lie on the side his change was in.

Looking back once I became an adult, I wondered how anyone could treat their own children like that! To let them go for days without food, heat, water, and electricity and have to figure it out for themselves. There was that one time we really started WWIII by successfully picking his pocket. But all we found was three white balloons which we blew up and tossed back and forth for a while. We left them there on the floor and when Mama woke up and was sober enough to recognize what they were, she asked us where we got 'em? She pretty much knew the answer—Daddy's pocket! She totally went ballistic! You'd think she was under some misguided impression that either one of them honored their marriage vows or something!

She cussed him for everything under the sun! She wanted to know, "Who is the little whore? You good for nothing, low down, son of a bitching whore-hopper!!!" It got worse. We tried to make ourselves scarce while she continued her rampage. She threw things, grabbed her blouse, and began ripping it off, the buttons went flying in all directions, she stomped what she couldn't rip or burn. There would be broken glass everywhere, torn pictures, ripped-up clothes. She'd even yanked the 10-cent plastic curtains off the window and used her foot to hold down one end of a curtain while she ripped upwards till it was shredded. We didn't have anything as it was, our entire house-hold was hand me downs, things other poor folks threw out, didn't have two matching plates or cups or silverware, and yet she always had to tear up and de-stroy what little we had. It was like some demon took over... she was pretty much always mean and pretty much always raising hell when she was sober, but the mere thoughts of him stepping out on her made her absolutely insane with jealousy! She was especially jealous during the early years. Forget all her bedfellows, her sleeping around wasn't even up for questioning, she was just on a mission, the end justified the means. That's nobody's business but her own and that's exactly how she saw it.

The neighbors on either side of us in Welsh Lane lived in single shotgun houses. To our right was two brothers living together, Hank and Tebbie Stewart. (Now that I look back at Mama's mispronunciations of just about EVERYTHING, I wouldn't doubt for a second that Tebbie's name was Toby Stewart or T.B. Stewart!). Anyway, to the left of us was a lady who lived alone named Ruby Stewart, and she was the sister of the two brothers. None of 'em had ever been married which I now find strange. Ruby wasn't particularly attractive or particularly ugly. She was short, slightly overweight, with short dark brown curly hair. But she did have one unique characteristic, she had black pubic hair that went clear down to the middle of her inner thighs and she liked to sit on her steps facing our steps with Bermuda shorts on and her legs spread wide if daddy was home. Evidently, she was very lonely and horny and thought daddy would find that sexy. I can't imagine any other reason unless she was just very proud of it. Sorta like a man being proud of the thick beard he grew maybe. Either way that was just plain stupidity, REALLY stupid, like if she blew her nose her head would collapse stupid.

Tebbie Stewart was short, chubby with a big round face and black hair and he was one of Mama's boyfriends, as well as a man named George Ivey who lived around the corner and up the alley a ways on Frank Street. There were a couple cops who stopped by to "visit" Mama also. One was named Johnny and he was very good looking. There was Uncle Red, (no kin), Randolph Gordon, (Mama's ex brother-in-law), Cottonbird, Harvey Hall and his brother, Kelly Hall and later Otis Padgett. I shouldn't call them her boyfriends, they really weren't, they were simply men who exchanged favors with her. Those are the ones we knew about. For someone who never left the house, she sure met a lot of men. It makes ya wonder if someone doesn't have a car, a phone, no computers back then and doesn't leave the house, what the heck did she do, send up smoke signals?

George Ivy was very tall and fairly broad-shouldered older man with white hair. He had a girlfriend named Juanita who lived with him off and on. She was right pretty and younger than he was. She had short black hair and very dark skin, maybe Indian descent. She was addicted to Terpin Hydrate, which I believe has Codeine in it and that was the cause of George Ivy throwing her out from time to time. She would come around the corner to our house and give one of us a dime or a quarter to go to the Lakeview Drugstore to get her some Terpin Hydrate. (Terpin Hydrate was a popular cough medicine for over a hundred years. It was an expectorant but it contained codeine, so it could become addictive. It was removed from the shelves of stores in the 1980s.) At first the stores got to where they wanted folks to sign for it and she couldn't get it as often as she wanted or needed it. She also was addicted to Paregoric which contains opium.

You could at that time buy it over the counter without sighing for it, but if you came in too often to buy it, they started asking questions. Anyhow she'd send one of us to the drugstore for her and sometimes she gave us a quarter! She was one of the ways we'd get some money to eat on. George Ivy came home from work one day and Juanita had sold every bit of his groceries trying to get money for her addictions. He threw her out for good then. Shucks... that was a sad day for us! When she gave us each a quarter, we could share a banana split at that drugstore. The best banana split I've ever had. It may have been 50 cents, can't remember exactly but it was cheap.

Hank Stewart was not one of Mama's boyfriends and I'm sure that was by his choice, not hers. Hank was taller than Tebbie and thin with light brown thin receding hair and wore glasses. He was the owner of the house he and his brother Tebbie shared and I believe he owned the one their sister Ruby lived in also. He seemed to be of a little classier than most of the folks around that neighborhood. It's like he was trying to make something of himself and maybe eventually get out of that area. That's the impression I get looking back anyway. He wasn't friendly but he wasn't mean either. Came across strictly business, almost on a mission all the time. Hank opened a hamburger café up on Broad Street just pass the top of the hill where the bridge went over the canal. He "once" gave us a free burger when we stopped in but only the one time.

They were absolutely delicious, or maybe it was just that we were so hungry at the time. I personally never went back into his café because if I had enough money for a burger, I would head to the What A Burger stand which was even a better burger. Hank's place was doomed from the start though, there was no place to park and Broad Street being a very busy street back then folks couldn't just stop there. They would've had to go park at the Frank and Broad liquor store and walk up to his café. Hank had a cream-colored Bulldog named Bozo. His yard was fenced in but Bozo got out when Brownie went in heat. We saw Bozo on top of Brownie and we ran over to defend Brownie! We thought she was being bullied by Bozo, having no idea of what was really going on. So, Bozo tried to exit too fast and became stuck. So here they were rump to rump and couldn't separate. We're all hollering and yelling at Bozo and finally Hank comes out the door and throws a bucket of cold water on them. Not sure now how quickly it happened but they did separate after that. I don't remember Brownie becoming pregnant again after Pearl Ave, so Bozo must've been shooting blanks.

When Mama sobered up, she'd stay sober for a week or two, maybe even a month. Then we usually ate pretty well, because one way or the other if Mama was sober, Mama's gonna eat! First thing when she got sober, she realized the lights and the water had been turned off. She would raise hell at daddy as if he's the only one who drank his pay away, like she had nothing to do with it. She'd send us down to Cooter's house on the corner of Frank and Welsh Lane, to "borrow" a bucket of water. Cooter was a heavyset middle aged black lady who had a garden in her backyard or somewhat of a garden anyhow.

She didn't grow a lot in it, maybe bugs ate it up as fast as it grew, I don't know. But Cooter had a spicket in her backyard that sat fairly low to the ground. We could just get a bucket under it and that's where she reluctantly allowed us to get the water. I hated to be the one Mama sent down there to ask for water. Cooter was none too friendly toward us and always had a sour look on her face when we asked, although she never said no. Of course. a lot of folks acted that way toward us knowing our parents were drunks and we were filthy low class heathens, apparently. I'm sure neighbors seen men going in our house when we kids and Daddy weren't home. I guess they figured Mama was a whore so we all must be little whores. And they dang sure had to hear all the fussing and fighting, hell-raising, and threats! Wasn't like our house was insulated or had double windows or sat far away from theirs. Heck, most of the time our windows were up! Us kids paid the price a lot more than they ever knew or cared.

Eventually, with the help of one or two "boyfriends," Mama got the lights cut back on, the water too. In the cold months, she would send a couple of us kids up to the EZ store on Broad Street for a Croker sack of coal, (that's the way coal was sold to individuals, a burlap type bag called a Croker sack) The sack was bigger than we were! Also, to get a glass jug of Kerosene from the Dixie Vim service station. She also put food on the table with the help of her boyfriends. Nothing too elaborate, Butterbeans and Cornbread, Kool-Aid, or Fried canned Corn Beef and Taters with light bread and syrup or a big pot of boiled Cabbage and some Sweet Potatoes with fried Cornbread. We seldom ever had any type of meat. Closest thing was fried Fatback, the grease from that seasoned the beans, but good Lawd, we was eating! We was happier than a butcher's dog! After cooking a few meals like that though, she'd get drunk again and stay that way for a month. Which as time went on turned into staying drunk for two months, then three months and daddy too. How the heck their bodies lived through that is beyond me! So, we'd be back to fending for ourselves again and it's a wonder we survived and even a bigger wonder that they survived all that drinking.

It seemed like Jewel and Judy was almost never home and Dale was gone frequently also. They would go to an aunt's home or Granny's or maybe a friend's house, if they had a friend. I never knew where they were. When any of them left the house if Joyce and I tried to follow them, they would turn around and tell us to go home, even run toward us like they're gonna hit us if we didn't stop following them. They had friends like Lutrell Howard and her daughter Maxine in the project. But whenever and wherever they went to, they would stay gone for days on end.

Whenever there was coal and or kerosene in the house, while Mama and daddy lay passed out right beside that pot-bellied stove, we kids would attempt to build a fire to get warm. More often than not it was just me and Joyce home with them passed out and we would wad up newspaper or those brown grocery sacks and place that in the bottom of the potbelly stove. We put coal on top of the papers, then strike a match and reach way down trying to light the papers all around. If the papers burned up before the coals were lit, then we'd pour the kerosene over it. Of course, we didn't know we shouldn't be pouring a flammable liquid over embers. Thank God it wasn't gasoline. We weren't a whole lot taller than the stove. We had those glass kerosene lanterns and we lit those too and carried them through the house and they were way too heavy for small kids to be trying to carry. Our kitchen stove was a three-burner stove with a glass jug you fill with kerosene and turn upside down on one end into a bowl shaped reservoir. It then dripped down into a pipe that ran along the front of the three burners. You had to lift the glass cylinder housing that covered the round wicks to strike a match to the wicks. Each burner had a knob to adjust the flame. So, if they were turned up the wrong way or too high, fire came shooting out the top. The problems was, you first had to turn the knob downwards to get the wick saturated with kerosene, and then turn it upwards before lighting. You couldn't tell whether it was too high until after you lit it which took both hands. One hand to hold a lit match to the wick while the other hand held the cylinder up. But if we could find something to cook or heat up, we did as far back as I can remember. Mama and daddy slept through anything we did, never knowing how closely they laid to danger.

Mama being sober had its drawbacks too! That meant school! She didn't care a hill of beans about our education or whether or not we went to school. Her only concern was her and daddy being arrested. After days of not being in school, suddenly we'd be woke up by that wide, thick Garrison police belt hitting us. "Get your asses' outta that bed and get to skoo! (It would be noon because that's when she woke up!) If Liz a-B

Hamilton comes knocking on that door you lil'sons a bitches, I'll ke'ya!" (kill). If we were awake enough to hear Mama getting up and heading our way, we'd jump up and get under the bed so she couldn't hit us with that belt. Then she gets the broom and try to hit us and poke us with it or wire coat hanger, whatever she could get her hands on that would reach us. Once she was that mad, I'd pity the grizzly bear that tied to tangled with her!

Here's what was really going on with that. She just sobered up, and she needs a boyfriend to come over to get the lights and water back on and some food before Daddy comes home. He may be at work, or staggered up to his mama's or may be in jail. It was always one or the other. But she needs us out of the house… doesn't matter if half the school day is gone, or that we have no clean clothes to put on, can't bathe, had nothing to eat, just get up and go. So, we'd mossy on outta the house toward an aunt's house or to Granny's. We went to school sometimes, but we played hooky a lot.

Neither of our parents ever encouraged us to attend school for educational purposes. Never once ask us anything like what we would like to be when we grow up, or suggest we may want to graduate High School one day. It was always, "Keep yo asses in school till you're sixteen, then I don't give a damn what ya do!" She'd say, I don't give a damn if ya get an A or an F, as long as ya know how much change you're 'pose to get back and ya can read the label on a canned good that's all ya need to know." She'd say, "You a damn girl, ya don't need an education to get married and have young'uns!"

Who with half a brain is gonna get up at the crack of noon or later and go make a grand entrance in their classroom where they're already shunned and ostracized and sneered at! Mama really expected us to get up in the freezing cold, nothing to build a fire with, try to "find" whatever stinks the least and is dry, not bathe or brush our teeth, nothing to eat no lunch money, just run a comb through our hair and go to school! Just to keep her from having to go to court! (Which we did have to do a few times). She didn't care about us enough to get us up in the mornings, feed us, clean our clothes, etc. but we're supposed to care whether or not she has to go to court.

The times we did have to go to court due to school absences, the entire family of seven walked all the way downtown to the courthouse, (I believe it was on Ninth Street). We sat there before Judge Hardin and listened to all the Blah, Blah, Blah, excuses Mama gave as to why we weren't in school on a regular basis.

"Well, Judge, it's like this, I get 'em up and get 'em ready and feed 'em and they head out to skoo and they decide to go someplace else instead. I've walked 'em to skoo personally, and waited till they all went in the buildin'. But they were goin' in one door and out the udden! I'd go home thinkin' my kids are in skoo all day and they didn't even go in their class. I've whooped 'em just about down in the floor and it ain't done a bit of good. My brotha is a insurance salesman and he's drove by 'em and saw 'em walkin' during skoo hours, heading for the Project to their Granny's or someplace. And even he's got out of his car and whooped 'em and threatened 'em. But if you'll give 'em another change their dead-ee's gonna pick 'em up in his cab and he's gonna drive 'em to skoo and go in wid 'em and march each one to their class and make damn sure they go in it."

All the while Elizabeth B. Hamilton, a Juvenile Court Officer, (but Mama called her a "visiting teacher") with her Coke-bottle glasses, bright red lipstick, and crazy blonde hair, would be up there standing right beside the judge and showing him papers and folders and whispering to him as she's pointing to different ones of us kids. Eventually the judge would say, he's gonna give Mama and Daddy one more chance and they had better get us in school and we had better stay in school!

(Come to find out years later, Elizabeth B. Hamilton and Judge Hardin were working together in the baby-selling business and the main reason we were placed in that old lady Cooper's home for children is she had planned to come get Joyce and sell her, back when Joyce was just three years old. The rest of us had already become too old for that. Soon afterwards they most likely figured Joyce too was past the age most couples wanted also).

So, after court, we all walked all the way home and Mama and Daddy would get drunk because they now had a "good reason"—as if they ever needed one—they were mad and embarrassed! LOL! AND it was our fault! We were Mama's little heathen sons-a-bitches and she never let us forget that. Sometimes Mama would stop at H. L. Greens and buy her some sugar-coated orange slices and or caramel coated nuts. She'd have them in a small white bag, which she hid when we got home. Not too many hiding places in a shotgun house and as soon as she got drunk, we'd find it and get a piece. We'd eat a piece and put the rest back.

Next day, we'd eat a piece and put the rest back always hoping she wouldn't notice when she sobered up. Eventually, we had eaten it all! It would be three or four weeks later and we done long forgot all about her candy when, all of a sudden, she'd be raising mortal hell! After a couple days of her being sober, I guess she went looking for her candy. We'd hear, "Well, I be a son of a bitch! I can't have a G** Damn thing for you little sons of bitches!" Sorry. Mama, we did get sorta hungry in the two months yaw been drunk....

It was somewhere in this same timetable that Judy came home from school telling Mama that her teacher whooped her or threaten to. That in itself would be rare because teachers generally sent students to the principal's office to be spanked. (I never heard of any student being spanked or paddled by a teacher and I had some very belligerent, trouble making boys later on in my fifth and sixth grade classes.) They were always sent to the principal's office to be paddled. Mr. Morrison, the principle, would have the student hold their hand out, palm up, and he would hold on to the tips of their fingers and bending them downward to stretch the skin tight and then he'd whack their hand with a wooden ruler. One to three whacks usually but good and hard. So, I really have my doubts that Judy was being truthful. She was in the fourth grade and I believe Ms. McCullen was her teacher. Lo and behold, here's Mama who absolutely hated to leave the house, couldn't care less if her kids ate, ran the streets day and night, burned the house down or blew it up, but with the attitude of, "by God, ain't no damn body gonna whoop one of my young'uns," she marched all the way to the school with Judy in tow. She stands outside Ms. McCullen's classroom window just a cussing and screaming and threatening to whoop HER ass. Ms. McCullen's class was in a separate building than the main school. It was a one story smaller building behind the main school. From what I understood as they told it, the building was locked when they got there but looking through the window of Judy's classroom, they could see her teacher still in there. Mama kept daring the teacher to come out and get her ass whooped. Of course, she didn't. But what we learned from this is, no matter what we did in school, we weren't gonna get paddled for it because our Mama said so! Mama out there hollering, "If one of my damn young'uns needs a whooping, you tell me and I'll whoop 'em, but there ain't no damn body else better whoop 'em!" (That's a real bad message to send to your kids. After I grew up and had kids of my own, I said just the opposite. I told my sons if they got paddled in school and I found out about it, when they came home, they'd get another one.) But that was the Loraine Palmer's way. She considered herself the star of this show and everyone else were just extras and ain't no damn body gonna step on the star's toes!

We had a "slop jar" under one of the two double beds (where the five of us slept) to pee in should we ever actually wake up during the night before peeing in the bed… we didn't. But we used it during our waking hours, day or night, especially in the winter months because the bathroom was so cold and, of course, when the water was shut off for nonpayment. (Mama and Daddy had their own "slop jar" under their bed. She had a folded newspaper sitting on top which served two purposes. It was reading material and a lid. Add that to the other odors in our house)!

The bathtub was against an outside wall, and where the floor met the wall, there was about a two-foot high by four-foot long section of wall missing. Rotted away, due to unpainted wood, and a big fig tree just on the other side of that wall so no sun could get to the wood to dry it out. Plus, the fig tree hid the hole in the wall from the outside. We didn't realize that until one night Randolph Gordon came in and was sleeping in the kitchen floor. When asked how he got in, he said he crawled in under the tub! He had come to our house many times and slept in the kitchen floor, he probably noticed the hole under the tub when he seen daylight coming from under it while still laying in the floor one morning with the bathroom door open. But we now knew why it was so frigid cold in there!

Rats came in too, big rats! We use to lie in bed and watch them scurrying around in the kitchen. If there happen to be any bread or anything we could feed them, we did! We threw out pieces of bread or whatever

Mama's Slop Jar after we kids were all grown and moved away. In this house on Wrights Ave, her bathroom was right next to her bedroom and the slop jar no longer fit UNDER her bed! Yet she wanted it right there!

we had at the time and watch them run over and eat it. Mama found a nest of baby rats in the wall under the kitchen sink. She dug them out of there, they were pink and hairless, and then she poured boiling water over them. Dale was just a crying and begging Mama not to kill the babies. We thought Dale must be crazy to want them to live! Mama told her to shut the hell up or she'd give her something to cry about. After killing all the babies, Mama nailed a piece of tin over the opening in the wall. She'd save the empty cans from canned goods to use for that reason and they were also her spittoons for her snuff spit. If we ever learned anything from her, it was how to be low-class rednecks. LOL

Like I previously stated, our heat source was a big black potbellied stove that was right beside Mama and daddy's bed in the living room. When Mama was sober and had coal, she would build a fire so hot that that pipe that came off the rear top of the potbellied stove, and connected to the wall would glow orange! Daddy was always fussing about how hot she had their room as soon as he came home. (He should've tried sleeping in the bathtub where it was icy cold!). One time while she had that pipe glowing orange, she began accusing him of messing with other women or some such, we rarely paid much attention to what they SCREAMED at one another since they raised hell 24/7 if they were both home and sober. But she picked up the fire poker and started hitting that pipe! It was breaking it up after a few whacks and sparks were flying all over (in more ways than one!) Here we have unpainted wood slat walls and she has red hot cinders flying all over the room right next to their bed!!! It had to be a God intervention that the house didn't catch fire. But once she was mad, she didn't care what she did or who she hurt. I believe that was the time she found an unused but unwrapped condom in a small matchbox he had in his pocket. Obviously, for quick and easy access! There was no doubt he fooled around with other women, he knew he was good looking and he liked the ladies. But now all her "boyfriends" were a different story, she had good reasons… like getting the electric and water turned back on or paying the rent or getting some food in the house and of course the boyfriends must always buy her some liquor or wine…. In her mind, she was totally justified to sleep with as many men as it took. But she was extremely jealous of daddy the whole time we were growing up, to the point of insanity almost. I guess had he also charged for his services it would've been okay. Once things calmed down some from the initial fight that sent her into a poker wielding frenzy, she starts raising hell again telling daddy he best be figuring out a way to fix that stovepipe because she's cold!

Before someone gave them that potbelly stove and they had to actually use the fireplace for heating that room. On the mantelpiece over the fireplace was an 8x10 framed picture of daddy in his Marine uniform

on one side and on the opposite side of the mantelpiece was an 8x10 framed pictured of Mama's first
husband, Fred McDonald, in his Army uniform.
Mama would constantly throw Fred up to daddy, saying things like, "I wish you had died instead of Fred,
you're not half the man he was, I wish I was still married to Fred then I would've never met you, you low
down good for nothing son of a bitch!" If I had a
nickel for every time I heard that or something like
that, I'd owned the bank! I don't recall daddy ever saying much back to her when she compared him to
Fred. Maybe he didn't know the truth about Fred
McDonald but I found papers that revealed quite a bit
about him. He was 5'7" tall with black hair, dark complexion. He enlisted in the Army in June of 1940 and
was listed as a cook. Four months after enlisting, he
went AWOL and was missing for three months and
sixteen days. When they found him, he was sent to
Fort Leavenworth and imprisoned for 387 days. He
was court-martialed and given a dishonorable discharge. What's weird is his Army records list him as
Clarence McDonald no middle initial. His marriage
license to Mama list him as Fred McDonald, (she always said his first name was Clarence but he went by
Fred), and the cemetery has him listed as Clarence E.
McDonald. (Born 09-15-1919, Died -01-11-1944) I
guess they meant F but they have his middle initial as
E. He was a drunk, a gambler by profession and had

Here is just a few of the pictures she burned or marred...

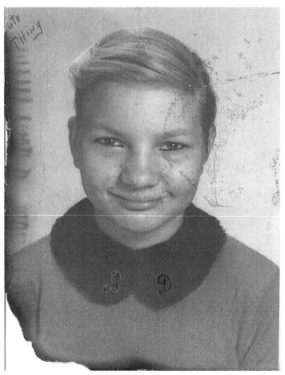

Tuberculosis. He was only twenty-four years old when he died. Mama met and married him inside of five and a half months. They were married one year and four months when he died. But this is the guy she constantly threw up to daddy as her knight in shining armor.

She would take the pictures of daddy and the pictures of us girls and throw them in the burning fireplace! Daddy would snatch them out real quick. She burned, marred, or totally destroyed many pictures through the years. She marked pictures with ink pens, stab them with ink pens and ripped many of them up. Here are the two pictures that were on the mantel of daddy and Fred.

They never paid for any of our school pictures, IF, we happen to be at school on picture day to have even them taken. We had to tell our teacher's the pictures fell down behind the mantel into the wall. Yep, ALL FIVE packets fell down behind the mantel! "If 'en you don't believe it, just go ask my mama!" I only recall seeing a couple different school pictures of each one of my sisters till this day. Most likely she threw the entire packages in the fire. Daddy may have been shell-shocked, but Mama was plainly a mental case, period.

We met a girl in the alley one day named Helen Lowe. She was a cousin of the Master's family next door to us. She was tall and thin and had long black hair to her waist that she kept tied back in a ponytail.

She had wispy bangs and a few freckles across her on either side of her face. I thought she was so beautiful. Every time I'd see her, she'd be standing there talking to one of my sisters and I'd run over there too and just stare at her. If anyone remarked on her beautiful hair, she'd say she hated it and wanted to cut it off but her old Indian daddy would beat the mess out of her if she did. I thought, why would she hate it, it's so beautiful! I heard that when her daddy passed away, she immediately cut her hair off. I just thought it was weird that a parent would care what ya did with your hair Maybe that made such an impression on me because my mama whacked my hair off just shy of looking like she used a bowl for guidance. She always cut our bangs too short but she didn't cut off my sister's hair like she did mine. Here's a picture of the four us of, I'm the one

with the bowl cut. And here's my second-grade school picture. Even when she didn't cut my hair off really short, she would whack it all up.

Back Row left to right: Dale, Judy, Joyce, and me in the shorts. Rarely did Judy ever smile throughout our childhood. Her expression was always one of anger or distain and she seemed to hate daddy, her sisters, well except for Joyce, and the entire world! The other four of us laughed and cut up all the time. Whether we were hungry or even when we just got beat ten minutes before, the next thing you know we were being silly and laughing. We all had daddy's sense of humor and personality while Judy had Mama's "no laughing allowed" personality. Maybe Judy just took life harder than the rest of us. She seemed to absolutely purely hate Daddy and defended Mama. I never understood that.

I've always believed my mama went out of her way to make me look the worse. Pictures are evidence. I've always known my mama hated me the most, but I never knew why. Judy told me ever since I was old enough to understand a sentence and throughout my life that Mama gave me to her sister Edna, who was married to Randolph Gordon at the time. Here are pictures of when I was with my Aunt Edna. She dressed me up and bought me a stroller. She walked all over downtown showing me off. Everyone denied that I was given to Aunt Edna later but Judy never backed down from that story and reminded me of it up until the time she passed away. Judy said the only reason my Aunt Edna brought me back to Mama's is because she was divorcing Randolph who turned into a drunk who wouldn't get a job and she could no longer keep me. Randolph would only wash windows downtown for store fronts where he was paid in cash daily, and then he'd drink up whatever he made. The story does fit because Mama told me all my life she hated me, and in more ways than just words. I didn't hate her; I simply felt nothing one way or the other toward her. The things Mama said to me use to hurt me deeply and broke my heart when I was very young, but over the years I became calloused to it.

We girls frequently went out scouting for drink bottles. Coke, Pepsi, RC, 7-Up, Upper 10, Bubble Up, Root Beer, didn't matter, you'd get 2 cents back per bottle.

Walking up back alleys we were always looking toward the back porches of other's homes to see if we spotted any drink bottles. If we did, we'd go around and knock on their front door and ask if they had any empty drink bottles we could have, and of course 99 percent of them said no. We knocked on the front because we didn't want them to know we had already seen the bottles they had sitting out back. Not trying to sound like a goody two shoes or anything but I flat refused to go in their yards and take their bottles. But I sure waited in the alley just outside their yards while Dale ran up, grabbed the cartons, and ran back to the alley. She'd hand them to me and Joyce grabbed the rest of 'em and off we'd go running as fast as we could. So, I was just as much a thief by being an accomplice to stealing but couldn't bring myself to ever actually do the stealing. I believe because I was so fearful someone would open their back door and catch us! Dale was much braver than I was. We'd rush to the EZ Market there on Broad Street and get the money for the bottles. Right next door was the What-A-Burger stand. The best Hamburg's in the world! There were times we had enough to get us each a hamburger and a milkshake even if we had to make two trips in search of empty bottles. We were in hog heaven for sure!

Once we were walking pass the back of the EZ Market and a delivery truck pulled up in back there delivering RC's. The driver got out and loaded cases of drinks on a dolly and rolled them into the store. Dale got two of the six pack cartons and ran toward Chaffee Park. After we got up the street a ways we sat on the curb and popped the tops off by pressing the cap against the curb and hitting the cap on top with the palm of our hands. It must've been 100 degrees in the shade that day and those drinks were even hotter it seemed. But we were so hungry and we loved carbonated drinks! After drinking or I should say guzzling, two or three each, we began to feel very, very sick. We threw up all the way home and vowed to never drink another hot soda.

We generally were barefooted out there in that heat. I remember making quick dashes from one little patch of grass to another. And crossing parking lots we'd make a mad dash to any little spot of shade we could see to cool our feet off. Crossing roads was the worse, especially Broad Street where the metal rails were still intact and running in both directions from where the old trolley cars use to travel. We found out quick, pay attention to the rails!

Daddy absolutely loved going down to the Bell Auditorium to watch the wrestling matches. Especially if it was a tag team match or if his favorite wrestlers were gonna be there. It was usually on Monday nights. He didn't want to go by himself for whatever reason, so he'd take one of us kids with him. Jewel claims Mama made daddy take one of us because she didn't believe he was actually going to the wrestling match. That's very possible since she was so jealous of him. Jewel said she went with him sometimes. I remember he took Joyce usually, and I only remember getting to go once. I really wasn't interested in the fights but loved that I got to go someplace with daddy and he bought me some popcorn. Daddy would buy himself a quart of beer or a pint of wine. He had it in a brown paper bag and sipped it with the bag still over it. Maybe they didn't allow drinking in there and that was his way to sneak a drink but usually by the time they were heading home, he was getting pretty well lubed up. I don't know how many times or even if Dale got to go but I know for a fact Judy never went with him, she wanted no part of him for any reason. No one could convince daddy those wrestling matches were staged. He'd get mad at the mere suggestion they were fake. He'd get his middle finger going, poking it down toward the floor over and over while he proclaimed he knows that he knows they're for real fights! He'd say, "You can't tell me they can fake that blood! I saw that blood start pouring out of his forehead myself! Uh-Uh, Uh-Uh, Uh-Uh, don't try to tell me cause I know! I've done seen too many fights now and there's no way they could fake the ones I go to! You mean to tell me you don't think that's real?" LOL! He was so funny once he was sure he was right about something.

Mama was never interested in going any place with or without him. She would not go visit his mama or sisters or even hers for that matter. Daddy was always the one who went to the store their entire marriage to buy any grocery items. I bet I could count on one hand how many times she has ever been in any store. When they were sober, he liked getting up early, listening to music on the radio while he drank a cup of coffee, and wrote a letter to someone, like his brother David who lived in Indiana or his other brother Herbert who was usually in prison for thief. When we had coffee, it was always one of those little jars of instant coffee. He would then usually leave and walk somewhere like up to his mama's or sister's. Anywhere, he loved to go even though he had to walk. Mama on the other hand didn't even begin to rouse before noon or one pm. She hated music, she hated all the kin folk, and she hated leaving the house. She was a TV person. She loved *Perry Mason, Dr. Ben Casey, Dr. Kildare, Gunsmoke, The Alfred Hitchcock Hour, The Outer Limits,* and her most favorite was *The Untouchables with Elliot Ness.* She pretty much didn't care what anyone else did or where any of us were, as long as she got to watch her shows uninterrupted! We usually had one TV on top of another. TV's that others had thrown out because the sound or picture didn't work. So put one of each on top of the other and you have a complete TV. My daddy wasn't too much a TV fan period. Red Skelton Show and The Three Stooges were the only ones I remember him liking very much.

Daddy loved to play his guitar and sing to anyone willing to listen. He loved to sit on the front porch, that way the neighbors could hear him too. LOL The bigger his audience the better he liked it. Of course, Mama didn't care to hear that either! Heck, she didn't care to hear Johnny Cash or Hank Williams, she sure didn't wanna hear Ed Palmer! Of course, when we were kids daddy never had a guitar for long. He always ended up pawning it, (for drinking money, I have never heard of him pawning it for grocery money). It was only after all us kids were grown and left home that he kept a guitar for any length of time.

Before he passed away, he had a Martin guitar and he talked about that thing being his most prized possession and how he's wanted one all his life, how good it sounds and on and on and on. He pawned it… loss that one too. He had a cheap junky guitar when he passed away but at least he had one which is more than I can say while we were growing up. We kids loved nothing better than to sit out on the porch with him listening to him playing and singing. (Except Judy, she hated anything and everything he did). That was one of the few things we enjoyed at home and yet he always managed to get rid of his guitar.

We never had a birthday party or even a birthday gift or a Christmas present growing up. In fact, I don't ever recall once my mama or daddy even saying "happy birthday" to me or my sisters. I was born on Mama and Daddy's anniversary, March 16, and all she ever mentioned was it's their anniversary. But one year in the fall, two ladies came to our house and asked Mama a bunch of questions about where Daddy worked and how much he made and such. I believe one of my sister's school teacher's put the Palmer name in for Holiday help with the Tuttle Newton Home if my memory is correct. Then one of the ladies leaned forward and asked Mama something, and Mama made us all go into the kitchen. Looking back now I assume we had to leave the room while the ladies asked questions like, what size this child wears and what she likes, for each of us. (Pfft, as if Mama would know what any of we liked).

Come Christmas morning, totally unbeknownst to us, they had brought in Christmas presents. We woke up and found a decorated Christmas tree in the living room. There was a bicycle for Dale and one for Judy, puzzles, coloring books, and crayons, Jacks, Ric-Racks, skates for Joyce and me, stuffed animals, and we each got a red mesh stocking filled with candy and nuts. Like the mesh onion bags are made of. I received a puzzle of the United States; all the pieces were hard plastic and yellow, red, and blue. There were tiny little flags to stick into a tiny hole that marked where the capital was for that state. I must've worked that puzzle 100 times during the next few weeks.

Then, we were told to go look under the beds. There was a very large box for each of us under our beds. When I opened mine, I couldn't believe it! I had a navy-blue pleated skirt and a white blouse with lace around the collar. Also, I had a white full slip, a couple pair panties. I don't recall any shoes, but I wore that skirt and blouse every single day for weeks and weeks on end. I had never owned clothes that were brand-new and bought just for me, that I could ever remember anyways. I was eight then and now I'm seventy years old and I will never forget that Christmas or how I felt. It was the happiest day of my entire childhood! I wished I knew who those ladies were when I grew up enough to contact them and tell them what that meant to all of us kids. But of course, Mama didn't have a clue how to contact them or how they chose our family. They had also brought in big boxes of food to make a Holiday meal. Usually even when Mama bought the stuff (or one of her boyfriends did) to cook Thanksgiving or Christmas dinner, she got drunk part way through it and never finished making it. But I sure hope God blessed those ladies and if they're in heaven right now, hopefully the good Lord told them what their actions meant to the Palmer girls. I don't ever recall a decorated Christmas tree before or after that one.

We sisters loved to mess with Mama and daddy though. Once we painted his fingernails red while he was out cold. We did not even KNOW about nail polish remover let alone own any. The nail polish was probably Jewel's or Judy's since they were old enough to babysat for aunts and earn some money every now and then. Or it may have even been something that was stolen. But we spotted it and put it to good use. He went to work driving the cab with those red nails! He had to explain to every single customer every day why his nails were red. Even when they didn't ask, he didn't want folks to think he wears nail polish so he would tell'em his kids played a joke on him. And once we painted Mama's entire nose green with a marker pen. She was so funny looking!!!! She didn't take a joke as well as daddy did. She raised mortal hell once she was sober enough to look in a mirror.

Daddy got arrested many times and was sent to the stockade up passed the projects or rather Ohmstead Homes. He got arrested for driving the cab drunk but also when he was just walking down the sidewalk. Even when he wasn't drunk! There were two cops in particular that loved to take him in. Every single time Broadwater or Tuten passed Daddy while he was walking someplace, they arrested him. I remember Daddy saying plenty of times he hadn't had a drink and yet they took him down for public intoxication. We would walk the stockade to see him. It was a fairly long walk from Welsh Lane, but we were use to walking a lot. We would cry when we saw him in jail and have to walk away and leave him there. But truth be told, he probably liked it!

They always, always put him in the kitchen to cook and he could eat till his heart's content. He usually knew some of the other men in there and he could catch up with what they've been doing, read his True Detective magazines and didn't have to listen to Mama. Heck, he didn't have a care in the world! He had electricity, warm water, food, heat… we were the ones suffering doing without those things. We didn't realize back then that he probably didn't mind one bit being locked up for the short periods they kept him, probably just a few days to a couple weeks. He never knew how emotional it was for us kids feeling so sorry for him.

One night while Daddy was spending a couple weeks in the stockade hotel, Mama I guess was starved for attention. So, she opened the front door and propped open the screen door with a kitchen chair and then ran out on the front porch screaming bloody murder! "CALL THE PO_LEESE, HELP, HELP CALL THE PO_LEESE!!!" Hank and Tebbie Stewart next door were the only ones who had a phone and they did call the police. The police came and Mama was telling them this black man named Tyrone something or other, broke in, went to the kitchen, and brought back a chair and propped open the screen door and leaving the front door open in case he had to run, and then proceeded to try and rape her! She said she told him to wait a minute while she closed the door to our room so as not to wake her kids.

Stockade 425 Wood St Augusta Ga

He allowed her to get up and instead of heading toward our room she made a beeline to the porch and started screaming. She said he hit her shoulder with his as he ran past her to escape. The police questioned the man and found he had an airtight alibi. They told her it couldn't have been Tyrone, so it must've been a different man, but she was emphatic that it was Tyrone so of course they surmised she made the whole thing up. You'd think she would've been arrested for filing a false police report, not to mention actually blaming someone by name, but they didn't do anything to her. She loved reading the newspaper when she was sober so I bet ya money she read his name in the paper because she certainly didn't know him. The woman never, ever, ever went anywhere except those couple times she had to go to court. She seldom even went out on the porch! She did not ever go visit anyone, or go to a store, daddy always went or she sent us kids. But with Mama, there's nothing like a little Palmer Drama to break up the monotony.

We came walking up the ally once and there was a police car in front of our house. One of us said, "Uh-oh, now what?" But when we got to the porch, there sat a police officer, with Mama, snapping green beans. That's when we first met Johnny. He sure was good looking! He brought Mama a mess of green beans and helped her "snap 'em," as we called it. That's breaking off the skinny ends then breaking the rest in half. We knew why he came to see Mama bearing gifts. We just couldn't figure out what someone who was as good looking as he was would see in Mama who always had a big dip of snuff in her mouth, her belly looked like she was pregnant and she usually stunk.

There was a Fish Store on Broad Street and the back of it was almost directly in front of our house across the ally. So, Joyce and I, and if I'm not mistaken Dale may have been with us that day, was walking down Broad Street and we stopped and went in that Fish Store. No reason, other than to check out what was inside. I cannot even stomach the smell of fish of any kind or seafood. But we still wanted to check it out. Inside were white cases with clear glass rounded tops, much like you see in the Deli section of a grocery store. They were filled with crushed ice and had whole fish lying on the ice. Still stunk to me! That was the first time I had ever seen a dead fish complete with tail and eyeballs.

Most of them were covered in dark gray scales and white around the head area. So freaking ugly... Ugh! That was the only thing in their store, Fish and crushed ice. The guy behind the counter was a heavy-set man with black curly hair and asked, "What'll it be?" We said we were just curious and came in to look at his store. He joked around with us for a while and made us laugh a lot. He said his name was Dan so we began laughing while saying, "Dan, Dan, the fisher man." (That was probably me since I make rhymes of everything.) I don't remember how this came to be or what he said to convince us, but he wanted to know if we wanted to ride somewhere with him and his buddy, who was working in the backroom, in his red pickup truck. It never occurred to us they could be perverts with ill intentions or to question why would they want to take three little girls whom they'd never met before some place with them! We just assumed they were being nice to us and we were excited to take them up on the offer. (And I don't recall anything about what the other man looked like or his name.)

Heck, getting to ride in a vehicle of any kind was exciting since our parents never owned one. I have no idea where they drove us to or why, I just know we three girls climbed in the back of their pickup, they locked up the store, and away we went. No one knew where we were or who we were with. They drove us out a pretty long ways and we were on a long dirt road full of potholes. I can't remember seeing anything but open fields and red dirt. I was sitting down just behind the back window of the truck and every time they hit a pothole it hurt my butt. So, I thought I'd get up and walk to the rear of the truck bed and sat there and maybe it wouldn't hurt so much.

As soon as I stood up, the momentum made me run and flip out of the truck. My hands went on the tailgate and I flipped right out onto the road with no control whatsoever as to what my body was doing. Dale and Joyce began screaming, "Gloria fell out, hey, Gloria fell out!" They stopped the truck, walked back to where I was, I got up and they saw I was okay, just startled some. I climbed back in and they drove off. After a while, they turned around and drove us back to the store. We got out, said, "Bye yaw," and walked away. Maybe they were just being nice to us because they never tried anything or even said anything out of the way toward us. But I have many times looked back and wondered if they had other intentions but changed their minds. It's crazy and it's scary to think what could've happened to us that day. Not a living soul knew who we were with or where we had gone. It never once even entered our minds that they may be up to no good. It's one of the times I now know there were prayers being said over us girls. Mama and daddy never warned us about talking to strangers or getting into a vehicle with someone we didn't know. Maybe no one's parents did back then. Abductions and child rape was almost unheard of, at least by us. I praise God for His Holy Protection!

BTW: The spelling of "yaw" is intentional because that's the way it's pronounced in Georgia. It's Tennessee or West Virginia where they pronounce it y'all and in Kentucky, they say, "You'ens." There are different southern accents throughout the southern states.

While living at Welsh Lane we use to hang out at Joe's Grill on Broad Street. It was a place a lot of the teens hung out in and played the Jukebox and danced. Of course, Dale and Joyce and I were too young to be a part of that scene but that didn't stop us. It was the "in" place to be so we went in. Closest thing to *American Bandstand* we ever knew and we loved being there. Joe Hutto, the owner, and his wife, had about six kids. The eldest daughter was seldom there unless she was in the back some place where we couldn't see her. There was Tony Hutto, Tyra Hutto, Wayne Hutto and a much younger brother and sister. Didn't know their names and seldom seen them in there. What's funny, we looked upon them two youngest ones as little kids who shouldn't be hanging around all those teens when Joyce and I were just as young as they were. I had a BIG crush on Wayne and Jewel has a big crush on Tony.

Tyra was so big and muscular he use to allow two teen girls to hang and swing from his biceps while he held his arms up. Buddy Tucker and Linda Beasley would come in, arm and arm and dance. We all jitterbugged to the rock n roll of the day from the jukebox. Awesome looking food too but we never really got any except for a couple times we had some French Fries. They served them in a napkin lined red plastic basket just like on *Happy Days* TV show! Mostly we just hung out and danced and got to smell the hamburgers and fries the other teens ate. Today's hang out spots for teens are mostly gaming I guess… more fun to dance and hear great music.

Meanwhile, the Master's family moved out and we never saw any of them again. Bless their hearts, they were every bit as poor as we were but at least their Mama wasn't a drunk. But that meant their side of the house was empty. Mama went in there and hosed it all down and swept the water out with a broom, attempting to cut down on the roaches. Trying to get rid of the head lice also I reckon. But word got around at Joe's Grill that it was empty and someone decided to have a party there! There was a live band called "King David" that was set up in the living room and the place was filled with teens. No refreshments, LOL, just music and dancing. Heck we might as well stayed at Joe's Grill. Not sure what that was all about or who initiated the party but it was fun solely because of the live band.

Later when my mama's daddy died, granddaddy's coffin was placed in the empty side of our house for viewing. Whoever was in charge I guess, brought in folding chairs, and set them up in rows across from the open coffin. Relatives came and went for several days which meant granddaddy's body was just on the other side of the wall from ours. I believe it was three to five days. Back then they did that sorta thing for whatever reason. Mama and her sisters would sit in front of the coffin for hours and hours and talk and talk about everything and everybody. I'm guessing it was to save on funeral expenses since no one had to pay for viewing services at the funeral home. It was creepy to me. I only remember going in there once for a few seconds. I didn't care for Granddaddy and Mama Hall and had no desire to be around them dead or alive.

At some point Jewel started hanging out with an older girl named J. Smith who was married and had a little boy. (I didn't spell out her first name to protect the innocent since her son is now a grown man) Jewel's personality changed and she began to act like J. Smith, or tried to, according to Mama. Jewel would probably deny she acted different but she did. She even dressed like her. They were both tall and thin and Jewel could wear her friend's clothes. Jewel became a smart-mouth belligerent and defiant brat. I mean worse than usual… She thought she didn't have to do anything she was told, especially go to school. (Of course, we all felt justified in not going to school.) Jewel use to say to Mama, "You witch, you witch, I'll put'a sssspell on you." She would say it in a joking way trying to sound funny. Well, we all cracked up and thought it was. The more she hung with J. Smith, the more Mama raised hell. I don't believe for a minute Mama cared a hill of beans where Jewel went or what she did. It was all about Mama and all about her controlling us (when she was sober). And according to Mama, "Jewel's actions were making HER look bad." (Now that's funny!) Mama's attitude was, "by God as long as you live under MY damn roof you will do what I ta'ya to do or I'll ki'ya!" Mama found out somehow that the two of them was seen more than once going into a hotel ran by a man named Earl Martin. Some say it was the Shirley Hotel but that doesn't ring a bell to me but it was a hotel of "ill repute" just the same. One day Jewel and J. Smith came to the house and I can't remember what started it but it was to do with that Earl Martin's hotel. The next thing I know I see Mama and Jewel fist fighting in the backyard. Mama had that Garrison police belt and was gonna give Jewel a whooping and Jewel grabbed the belt. Mama yelled, "Okay, ya lil' bitch, ya wanna fight like a woman then I'll fight'ya like a woman." And she took a swing at Jewel and then J. Smith jumped in and Mama was fighting the both'em. J. Smith had pierced ears and was wearing dangle earrings and Mama ripped her earlobe by pulling the earring downward. Maybe intentional or just happened during the fight, but J. Smith had blood on her shoulder and dripping down the front of her blouse. The police showed up and took Jewel in custody and then we heard the authorities had Jewel flown to the Atlanta Training School. She was fifteen when she went in and was there for a year and a half I believe. We're all home saying to one another, "Jewel got to fly on'a err-o-plane!" and "Did jew know Jewel went to Atlanta on'a err-o-plane?" "Wow, Jewel was on'a err-o-plane!" (Later, Jewel told us she puked in a bag on the plane. So we were saying to anyone listening, "Jewel puked on the err-o-plane!" "Did jew know Jewel puked in that err-o-plane?"). We were all such rednecks! The song "Don't Worry About Me" had just come out, it was 1961 and Jewel learned to embroidery while in Atlanta Training school and she embroidered that title onto a white table scarf along with flowers and leaves. It was real pretty and I wish one of us still had it. But when all was said and done, Jewel had a bad reputation from the whole Earl Martin thing. But she had no idea what happened in that place.

She said her and J. Smith would walk all over downtown Augusta. J. Smith loved to walk and loved to dance. J. Smith was a right pretty blond and always wanting to have a good time. Jewel didn't have any money but her friend did and she probably spent money on Jewel for burgers and such. Jewel said when they went to Earl Martin's hotel she was put in a room with a small black and white TV and was told to wait right there. J. Smith would leave and return in about half an hour saying, "Let's go" to Jewel. And they would leave. Jewel always thought J. Smith was her age or maybe a year or two older but J. Smith was in her twenties, not her teens. Jewel was only fifteen and that's probably what saved her from knowing what was going on. The ones running the "fun house" probably didn't want to chance having a minor providing "services" just in case they got busted. So they never informed Jewel what was going on let alone asked her to participate in anything like that. J. Smith didn't even tell Jewel she was married and had a little boy! Jewel found that out later and was shocked to discover that D. Smith, who lived in the same duplex and across the hall from our Aunt Emmie, was married to her friend J., Smith. Jewel said whenever she went to Aunt Emmie's she sometimes would see D. Smith and his little boy but never knew he was married to her friend and that's where J. Smith lived also. Jewel said she can't believe how naive and dumb she was back then. All of us Palmer girls thought we were grownups and wise and even though we did have to be the parents to our parents many times, we were so naive, dumb, and illiterate! It was never our own wisdom and maturity that got us through but the Holy Spirit and Devine protection due to the prayers of people like our Uncle Glynn and Aunt Shirley.

Footnote: Understand we spoke with a very pronounced southern drawl and very poor grammar. We often made one word of two, "Did you" became "did 'ja" or if we were dragging out the words for emphasis it became, "Did jew." Or "Can she go with you" would be said "tak'err wid'ja, wood'ja."

Chapter 6

So, while Jewel was in Alcatraz, I mean Atlanta, we moved to 1947 of Broad Street, brick row.

The doors were all unpainted wood when we lived there and the windows were shot, with the sills and casings being old unpainted gray wood. The bottom of the building was not painted white and neither was the front of the porches, they were just cement and the

banister across the front was wood, no railing on the steps. There were no porch lights, just a street light on the corner. There was a glass transom window above the doors, not the solid panel seen here. And I sure don't remember that much grass either! There was grass in between each porch and along the curbs but it was very sparse and you could always see more dirt than grass. Our door locks looked like these every place we ever lived. Everyone around there had a skeleton key so why bother to lock up. Most folks didn't bother locking their door back then, if they did anything they flipped that little slide lever.

All of us liked living on Broad Street a lot more than that back ally. We loved sitting on the front porch watching traffic. I was ten years old when we moved to Broad. There were lots of kids my age and older and we quickly got to know most of the neighbors and some were even kinfolk. The way the units were arranged on every porch was the two outer doors were downstairs units and the two enter doors were the upstairs units. We always lived upstairs because the rent was $27.50 a month for upstairs and $32.50 downstairs. The upstairs units were hotter in the summer but warmer in the winter. There was no central heat or air. It was huge compared to the shotgun house we had just left. There were two fireplaces in each unit, one in the living room and one in the largest front bedroom. Most folks placed a gas burning heater in front of the fireplace. Of course, Mama and Daddy put the potbellied stove in front of the living room fireplace and the other fireplace in the front bedroom was not used at all. It was covered up with a buffet table they suddenly acquired. Maybe it was left there by the previous tenant or someone gave it to us. The buffet was the nicest piece of furniture we ever owned, probably at least six feet long with a door on both ends and a couple of large drawers in between. That buffet is where four of us sisters put all our worldly possessions. We still never had pajamas or socks so our panties, shorts and shirts went in there along with our color books, crayons, Jackstones, or whatever we may have owned at the time while the top was lined with our "doctored" baby dolls.

Besides the buffet there were two double beds in there and a closet. The other bedroom that was in located in the front was very small. It had a single bed pushed flush against the wall and a very old dresser

The top of our Buffet cabinet didn't look quite as rough as this one pictured but other than that it looked pretty much like this. Most of the handles were missing which made opening the drawers or doors difficult.

with a round mirror and that's about all it would hold. It was gonna be Jewel's room when she returns from Atlanta Training School. I have no idea where the single bed and dresser came from. So, when entering our house from the front porch, there would be stairs straight up until ¾ ways up, then the steps curved to the right and at the top of the stairs, you'd be in a small hallway. To the right there were those two bedrooms; and to the left from the hallway was the living room which was fairly big. It had the white wicker sofa, an upholstered chair, the potbellied stove and the two stacked TVs sets on the left side of the room. On the opposite side of the living room was the door to Mama and Daddy's bedroom which was very small. It con-

Sad that almost everything two people owned was stored in this. And behind the little mirrored door, tucked under her clothes, was where she hid her candy, her nylons and her one tube of red lipstick.

sisted of a double bed and a chifforobe which contained most of their clothing. It looked just about like this one in the picture.

And straight through the living room was the kitchen which had a table, chairs in the middle. To the left was an old round top refrigerator that had a long handle on the left front ya had to pull to the right to open, and the three-burner kerosene stove. The sink was on the right and had a built-in drain board but it was open underneath with exposed pipes. There was a closet with shelves in the kitchen on the far-left wall. The bathroom was really laid out weird. Just pass the sink the room narrowed and there was a door to a tiny room with only the bathtub in it. It butted up perpendicular to the kitchen closet. So, as you entered the narrowing of the kitchen there would be a door to your left housing the tub. Straight ahead would be another door that leads to the landing coming up from the backstairs. The back stairs did a complete 180 degree turn and they smelled of very old wood. Old wood and plaster like you'd smell in a very, very old vacant house. Once you're on the landing there is yet another door straight ahead that has a toilet and sink. So, the bathroom was split up into two rooms with a hall and landing in between them, it was a very strange layout indeed. Each room had a bare light bulb hanging from the ceiling in the center of the room with a chain, or in our case, a string to pull it off and on. When our electric was on, don't mean we had a working light bulb in every room but generally we did in the kitchen, living room and the two front bedrooms.

I use to ask Joyce to go to the bathroom with me because it seemed so far away and was always dark back there. Plus, I had to pass those backstairs, which was always very dark and the backdoor was never locked. Not to mention there would be roaches in the bathroom usually. AND I needed someone to hold the kerosene lantern! There was no place to sit it down back there except the floor. Joyce would say no, she ain't going. She only thought that was her final answer! LOL… I would pick her up and carry her to the bathroom with me while she fussed and cried out for help!

But most times she would agree to go with me because she would need me to go with her and also she knew she was going anyway, either on her own two feet or mine, made no difference to me. We were scared of everything! Darkness, roaches, ghosts, ax murderers! Whatever we could imagine, it scared us.

I cannot recall those front steps though without remembering this episode. I came in from school one day when I was 10 years old. I was getting my report card out from between the pages of a book on my way up. I was pretty proud of it. Mama was sitting in her chair just around the corner from the doorway and she was sober!!! I handed her my report card to sign, hoping she would look at my grades and be somewhat proud of me. She snatched the report card from me and began to rip it to shreds! She yelled, "I'm not signing four damn reports cards! How many times I gotta ta you lil sum bitches to sign it yo-self!" It hurt my feelings so bad, I had to go to school and tell my teacher I lost my report card. After that, all future reports cards I signed her name on the back, stuck it in my desk and turned it in the next day without ever taking it home.

Mama and Daddy's drinking only got worse while we lived on Broad Street. I don't recall the water ever being shut off there but the electric sometimes was turned off. Possibly the water was included in the $27.50 per month rent. Daddy only received $19 per month from the government and they sure as heck wasn't about to give that to the landlord so I assume the fact that they had five kids kept them from being set out on the street for nonpayment, at least until they paid on it or caught it up.

Daddy started roofing with a man named Vincent Griffith. Don't know how he met Mr. Griffith and I'm sure Daddy wasn't a whole lot of help to him since Daddy didn't know much about roofing. Daddy brought Mr. Griffith to the house and introduced him to us all. Vincent Griffith was tall, dark, and handsome. He had huge muscles, a flat stomach, big knotty knuckles from roofing, black hair and a thick mustache. He looked like a force to reckon with but he was extremely kind and polite. When Daddy would get drunk and not show up for work, (Vincent lived just up the street from us a few houses pass the brick row), Vincent would give Daddy a couple weeks and then he'd come down to our house, drag Daddy out of bed, sit him in a kitchen chair, shave Daddy, make Daddy cup after cup of black coffee that he usually brought with him, and wouldn't let up until he had Daddy 75 percent sober. Then he'd tell Daddy, "Ed, you can't keep doing this. You need to feed these little young'uns, this ain't right. I'm gonna come back in the morning and you better be ready to go to work, you hear me?" Daddy would nod yes. Next morning Vincent would make Daddy go with him but he knew Daddy couldn't work. Daddy would have a hangover and be so sick.

Vincent would bring Daddy home come lunchtime but would pay him for the day because he knew we had nothing to eat there at the house. Vincent loved Daddy like a brother and it showed.

Daddy started bringing men home. Don't know where he met them, probably Frank and Broad Streets or Al's place but they were strangers to him and to us. Daddy would drag kitchen chairs into the living room for them; usually there would be three men. At times just two men and a couple times there were four men. Most of the time it was just Joyce and I, or Joyce, Dale, and I. Judy stayed gone and usually Dale was somewhere else also. Daddy and the men would sit there making small talk and drinking. Daddy would say, "I have five beautiful daughters" over and over. (Heck, we were just dumb and naive enough to believe our Daddy was bragging on us girls, that he really thought we were beautiful!) It made us feel good and we thought as long as our Daddy was there, we were safe. Problem was, after just ten to fifteen minutes of them sitting there, Daddy would get up and go to his bedroom and "pass out." We couldn't wake him or get him to budge whatsoever. The first time Daddy pulled this stunt; a very big man picked me up and sat me on his lap. He tried to put his finger up my shorts while saying, "What's this right here?" I jumped from his lap and ran through the front hall and into my bedroom and hid under the bed. Joyce followed right along with me. We could see the hallway from under the bed and would know when the men left the house. They were in there for a very long time it seemed. Mama was passed out in their bed before Daddy ever came home with the men. They finally did leave at some point and we ran out of the house and up to Aunt Mae's, looking for our cousin Ivy. Aunt Mae was Mama's sister and she lived on the far side of the next porch up, which would be six doors away. Ivy wasn't home but we told Aunt Mae we were scared of some men Daddy had brought home. She didn't say a word to us but her expression said a lot.

Aunt Mae had five kids of her own. Three girls and two boys, Ivy was her fourth child and he actually was just two or three years older than me. He was almost as big as a man, we thought of him as the "big" brother we never had since he had always stopped by our place since he was a tiny fellow no matter where we lived. Mae's husband walked out on her and their kids' years before. It was solely on her to provide for her and her five kids. She took in ironing, cleaned for folks, and stopped in an elderly lady's home she attended to every day. She made enough to keep her family fed, pay rent, buy them school clothes and supplies and keep her utilities on.

Aunt Mae dipped snuff but she never drank alcohol of any kind. She made the best sweet tea and biscuits this side of Georgia. And when she had accumulated enough leftover biscuits, she made a chocolate bread pudding to die for! She would every now and then call out to me or Joyce or Dale from her front porch asking if we wanted something to eat. She NEVER had to ask twice! We ran over there as fast as we could and she'd give us a plate of beans and biscuits and sweet tea, and even chocolate bread pudding too when she had it! Why I was happier than a kitten full of cream. She had no idea how much that meant to us, especially since we had never heard the words "thank you" spoken in our house and most likely never said it to Aunt Mae or to anyone. (We were never ungrateful; we just had to learn good manners on our own once we grew up.)

Joyce was telling me how Aunt Mae came upstairs to our house once and she was madder than a hornet! I wasn't home to witness this, but I wish I had been. But I'm guessing it may have been as soon as Mama sobered up after us telling Aunt Mae about the men Daddy brought in. Joyce said Aunt Mae was so mad she even told Mama she wanted to whoop her ass! Mama was either very sick with a hangover or scared of Aunt Mae since Mama wasn't the type to be told off by anyone! Maybe the two of them had fought when they were teenagers and Mae whooped Mama but for whatever reason, Joyce said Mama just sat there quietly while Aunt Mae yelled and told her just what she thought! Even though we lived only six doors apart, Aunt Mae never came to our house and Mama never went to hers. So, it had to be something weighing very heavy on Aunt Mae's mind to even bother with Mama. Of course, nothing changed, nothing ever did.

So, Daddy continued to bring men in and tell them he has, "five beautiful daughters" then suddenly he was passed out dead to the world within ten to fifteen minutes, leaving the men there for us kids to fend off. He was sober enough to walk home from wherever he picked these men up, walk up our steep stairs; and carry chairs in from the kitchen for them, but couldn't possibly stay awake past fifteen minutes. I'm thinking he made a deal with the men in exchange for liquor, something like, "If you can get any of my daughters to have anything to do with you then its fine whatever they'll agree to, just don't hurt or rape them." But in all honesty, that's what I'm picturing happened.

He may not have even said that to them, no warnings, no restrictions, since he would have no way of knowing what they did to us or forced on us, and he obviously didn't care. Once again, prayers spoken over us girls no doubt saved us from a horrible outcome! And as dumb and naïve as we may have been, we weren't dumb enough to stay within reach of the men again. We would run up the street and get Daddy's boss Vincent Griffith. Boy, he would come down there and clean house within a minute. He was very polite at first and would say to the men, "Mr. Palmer has retired for the evening so you fellows need to say good night now." IF they didn't immediately start getting up and

Our Sweet Aunt Mae

Cousin Ivy and Cousin Eugenia at a
family reunion 2014

Eugenia was mine and Joyce's singing partner back in early 1960s. Eugenia
and her older sister Melvis, on Broad Street the way it looked back then.
Tuten's Grocery store and Al's liquor store across the street. She's standing
beside the steps to our porch. Eugenia was born one year after me and one
year before Joyce so this picture of her gives an idea of how young we were
when we moved to Broad Street.

moving toward the door, he didn't tell them twice. One big dude just sat there, Vincent snatched him up by the back of his shirt and the seat of his drawers and stopping just at the top of the stairs he asked, "Now you wanna walk down these stairs or go down 'em head first?" Of course, the guy was more than ready to leave on his own accord. We grew to love Mr. Griffith; he was always such a blessing to our family. He'd say to us on his way out, "Now you girls come down and lock up the door as soon as I close it and if you need me again, come get me." I don't know if he ever had a private conversation with Daddy concerning the men, but I can't imagine he didn't. If Vincent Griffith wasn't home, we'd run get cousin Ivy. Poor Ivy having to tell those men to get up and leave and he was just a kid himself. They could've hurt him but we never thought of that. We assumed if a guy told them to leave, they simply would. Ivy frequently stopped in just to "visit" for a few minutes. I believe he was checking in to make sure we're okay. We love Ivy and will always think of him as our brother. Joyce was eight then, I was ten, and Dale was twelve so Ivy must've been about twelve, maybe thirteen then.

I would love to tell you what a typical day was like in our family but there were no typical days. Lord only knows from day to day what would happen next. The only typical part was Mama and Daddy was usually drunk. When Daddy finally sobered up, he'd have a hangover so bad that he walked the floors day and night. He would beg God to please let him get over this one, to please let him live, to survive one more time and he promises to never drink again. I'm sure he meant it at the time, but we all knew and surely God knew it would not be the last time. Daddy didn't usually smoke unless he had a hangover, then he smoked one cigarette after the other. Sometimes after walking the floor for two to three days, he would go into the DT's.

(DT's means Delirium tremens: A central nervous system symptom of alcohol withdrawal that is seen in chronic alcoholism. Symptoms include uncontrollable trembling, hallucinations, severe anxiety, sweating, and sudden feelings of terror. DTs can be both frightening and, in severe cases, deadly. It occurs most often in people who have a history of alcohol withdrawal. It is especially common in those who drink four to five pints of wine, seven to eight pints of beer, or one pint of "hard" alcohol every day for several months.)

I remember once while Daddy was going through his withdrawals and had been walking the floors, coming into my room and waking me up in the middle of the night. I slept closest to the doorway so that's why he chose me. He kept asking me to come look out the living room window, which overlooked the backyard, and see if I see what he sees. I kept saying. "No Daddy, you know there's nothing there, please leave me alone." But he was persistent and said, "If you say you don't see anything, I'll believe it's my imagination and then I'll leave you alone." So, I got up and went to the window. He hadn't told me what he had seen, only wanted to know what I see. I looked and then did a double take! I told him I see a red ball moving across all the yards. It was probably the size of a soccer ball and it was glowing very bright red. There were fences between the yards, like wire fencing, short but too tall to step over and much too flimsy to climb over. There was a street light on the corner and enough light from the moon and stars to plainly see a person or at least see a silhouette of a person had someone been carrying the ball. Not to mention it was glowing red and there were no battery-operated LED lights back then. The ball went through the fencing of each yard all the way to the left until it reached just to the edge of our view. Then it traveled back to the right, straight through the fencing and as far to the right as we could see, then left again. He said he had been watching it do that for quite a while before waking me up. The ball also rose up very high, higher than any human could reach, then back down again. We watched it until we decided although we didn't have a clue what that was, at least it doesn't appear to be trying to get into the window. I never asked Daddy about that night or what he thought it could've been but I never forgot what I saw.

Daddy would finally begin to feel well enough that he would mosey on up to his mama's to get him something to eat. He not only would eat at his mama's or sister's house, he'd go into Kroger's and put a flat can of sardines in each of his hip pockets then go over to the luncheon meats, open a package of chopped ham, liverwurst, or baloney and take half the meat out, roll it into a roll and eat it on the way out. He left the partial package of lunch meat lying where he found it. Of course, the rest of us had nothing to eat and if the truth be told, he could see Mama was getting sober too so he'd make a beeline outta there. He didn't want to see or deal with the wrath of Lorraine.

He knew all hell was about to break loose and she would go on the warpath like an insane woman. It's almost like she found it strange the electric had been turned off, there was no coal to build a fire and there was no food in the house. How could she expect any different??? They had been drunk for two to three months straight and she somehow thinks us kids miraculously paid the electric bill and bought food! She'd cussed Daddy and called him every name except a sane man. He wasn't there to hear it, but that made no difference to her, the venom was gonna spew regardless! She busted up everything she could get her hands on, stomped things, ripped her blouse off.

For some reason she loved to hear the buttons go flying in all directions when she grabbed her blouse on either side and yanked! It became part of the Palmer drama with every meltdown! She'd be stomping around with her shirt wide open, her bra exposed, and in her pee-stained shorts looking for something else to break. We usually got outta there also because we knew she'd be lighting into us soon. If Daddy happened to return before her tantrum was over, oh my God! She really put on a show then! He done got his belly full some place and was feeling better and was ready to "stretch out a while" as he called it. Mama would be cussing and a fussing and fussing and a cussing and finally Daddy would say, "Woman, would you shut the hell up and STOP BEATING YOUR DAMN CHOPS!"

This sent her into a spasmatic conniption fit that would've shocked even Mama Hall! Then Mama would begin to threaten him, "I ta ya wut, I ta ya wut, you sum'bitch, I'm gonna leave you if it's the last damn thang I ever do!" Daddy would sit over there on the couch saying, "Watch'er, Watch'er," and then he would sound almost like he's growling it, "Watch'eeer, Wat-ch'eeer," and then he would say it in a real high-pitched, almost falsetto voice that he dragged out, "Wwwat-ch'eeer, Wwwatch'eeer, if that ain't the pure damn devil right there I don't know wut is! When that damn HALL temper starts coming out there ain't no tellin' wut she'll do! Woman if you don't stop beating yo damn chops I'm gonna gather up a few rags and head on up to my mama's or someplace!

God says it's better to live on a rooftop than with a contentious woman!" Any time he brought up the word or God she'd say, "Damn yo God! There ain't no God! IF there was a GOD, name one damn thang he's ever done for you!" Daddy would say, "Ahh-Umm, woman how in this world can you say sump'en like that? Why I would be afraid to even think such a thang! What in the hell is wrong wid'ya?" Mama would say, "I'll ta'ya wut's wrong wid me, I been living wid a low down good for nuthin' whore-hopping sorry sum'bitch like you for too damn long!" I cannot tell you when the first time was I heard Mama say those things, but I can tell you how hearing her say, "Damn yo God," penetrated my mind, spirit and heart like a dagger. And my mind has replayed them over and over and over and over throughout the years. I can still see her facial expression and the pure hate and anger she projected while saying them. It was bad enough what we kids done without but to be subjected to hearing words like that, to me, is the epitome of mental abuse.

I remember feeling so much dislike toward her, bordering on hatred and wishing she wasn't my mama. Their arguing continued with her telling him he better be finding a way to get some money and food while cussing him for everything she could think of. He would always return fire with, "I don't know where to get any money from, if you do then spit and give me a clue!" Then she's say, "I wish I could spit, spit on yo damn grave!" Then while plundering through the refrigerator and kitchen closet and finding nothing she would begin to cuss us kids. (Don't know what she expected to find after being drunk for two months and the electric turned off!)

She'd say, "Those little sum'bitches ate up every damn thang in the house. I wish every damn one of 'em would die!" And if she spotted one of us within eyesight of her, she would start telling us how she wishes we were never born and how she hates us. Daddy would say, "Lorraine, please don't cuss those little young'uns." This of course made her start in on him again… This same exact scenario, from start to finish, was played out many times over the years. We've heard it and heard it and heard it and heard it.

Dale said not long after we moved to Broad Street and she was twelve years old that she was laughing and giggling about something. I do remember she giggled a lot. But Mama having a hangover told her to shut it up. But Dale being Dale kept right on laughing out loud. Mama threatened to kill her if she didn't shut up. Then she picked up a crowbar, lifting it over her shoulder with the rounded part of the crowbar toward the back of her and threw it at Dale who ducked and it stuck in the wall right beside where Dale had been before she took off running. Dale said she got out of there knowing full well Mama was about to tear everything up.

It seemed we had a frequent turnaround of neighbors, at least the ones who shared the same porch as us. Maybe had something to do with all the Palmer Drama, who knows for sure? In the upstairs unit next to ours was a family named Hodges. They were an older couple who looked to be Indian with a granddaughter named Lucille who lived with them. Lucille was maybe fifteen years old, dark complexion, snow white teeth, short brown curly hair, a very pretty girl. She came out their door one day and sat on the banister that separated the porch and she was holding a pair of white leather tennis shoes. She seemed oblivious to us watching her as she began to lick the shoes. She licked every square inch of those shoes except for the bottoms. I asked her how come she's licking her shoes and she said she's licking off all the fresh shoes polish because, "it really pisses my granddaddy off."

Finally, her granddaddy appeared at the front door and ordered her inside. They must've moved out during the night because I never saw them again. Next to them in the downstairs unit were Bill and Nancy Williams. Bill was almost never home due to his job, so Nancy would invite some of us in to play cards with her. She had no children and seemed pretty lonely. She taught us how to play 500 Rummy and some poker games. Next thing I knew, they had moved away too. Strange how we never seen any families moving in or out, they simply appeared then disappeared! On the first porch to the right was a family named Heights. Besides the parents there were three daughters about our ages. It was so funny, the first time we met them and they introduced themselves to us. "I'm Pinchy, she's Tubby and she's Birdbrain." We laughed and asked if she was joking. Pinchy said her daddy nicknamed them all and that's what they go by. Pinchy because her eyes were so squinted you could barely see if her eyelids were opened. Tubby because she was chubby and Birdbrain because she was a scatterbrain, she said. We never knew their real names, or at least I didn't.

Every time they came off their porch and would be talking to one of us Palmer girls, one of their parents would come to the door and order them back inside. I assumed they didn't want their girls associating with us. Of course, it may have something to do with daddy passing out on the sidewalk just the other side of our porch! He almost made it all the way home, just couldn't get up the steps. There's nothing like stepping out your door and seeing your daddy 'asleep' on the sidewalk in the bright of day!

The next porch up to the left is where our Aunt Mae lived with her five kids and one more door up on the next porch was Mama Hall. Although she was Mama's Mama and our grandmother, she never once came down to our place in the three or four years we lived there. And I'm pretty sure Mama had never moseyed up to visit her Mama either! There was no love lost between them for sure. You've heard the phrase, like two ships passing in the night? Well, they were more like two empty cold hard freighters sitting idle in Antarc-

tica! We Palmer girls found out pretty quick we weren't welcomed to visit Mama Hall. The Brick Row did not have air condition, heck; I never even knew there was such a thing as air conditioners except for in stores, so some folks living in the downstairs units installed a screen door so they could leave their front door open in the summers. The only couple times I personally knocked on her screen door, I could see her sitting in her chair facing her TV in the living room. She looked toward the door and yelled, "Wut' ya want?" I said, "I come to see you." She grunted and moaned and grunted and slowly got outta her chair and came to the door and while LOCKING the screen door she said, "I'm watching my shows right now, you go play." Turned around and grunted her way back to her chair. She always had one of those small glass bottles of "Co-Cola" in one hand and a Kool cigarette in the other. She was probably afraid I wanted something to eat. (She didn't know us at all or she would have known we didn't ask people for food. We would go to their house in hopes they'd offer us something, but if they didn't, we left as hungry as we came.) Mama Hall only cared about Eugenia as far as I knew, based on what I'd heard. She helped Aunt Mae with Eugenia's school clothes and supplies and Christmas gifts, etc. I heard this years later so I don't know it as facts but I do know when Mama Hall wanted someone to run across the street to Tuten's Store to buy her some more Coca- Colas she'd first try to get Eugenia. She'd pay Eugenia a dime or a quarter to go, but if Eugenia wasn't around, she'd sit out on her front porch till she spotted Joyce or I. (Lord knows she wasn't about to go herself or walk down to our porch and call out to one of us… nope, she'd wait however long it took to spot somebody to send.) Then she'd give Joyce or me a nickel to go. Never, ever did she offer either if us a whole dime. Eugenia had a Mama who cooked and fed her family every single day without fail, she had school clothes and supplies and socks and a coat, etc. But the kids who needed it the most, and were every bit as much her grandchildren, were treated like cockroaches. She made no bones about not wanting us coming around. She was a gruff, mean old grouchy hag as far as I was concerned. I know Eugenia loved her dearly, but Eugenia had a totally different grandma in Mama Hall than we had.

When I was eleven, after one of Mama's tirades and her proclaiming how much she hates me, I packed up some clothes and left home. I went to my dad's sister's house in the project. Aunt Emmie said I could stay there for babysitting while she went to church and helping her clean the house. She was a fanatical house keeper and I helped her keep her black tiled floors shiny and spotless. She did most of the work though and it was hard to find something to do because she never allowed it to get messy to begin with. She had three sons and they were all easy to care for, well behaved and sweet. Her husband, Uncle Billy, only came home on weekends and every Sunday without fail, after she came home from church, we all went for a ride in his car. This was a family ritual and never deviated in any way. He would drive way out someplace, just driving around, and Aunt Emmie would see a farmhouse or a silo or a barn or a water tower, and she'd point and say, "Billy, what's that, sug?" (She always called him SUG, short for sugar.)

Uncle Billy would say, "I don't know, Mama." No other conversation whatsoever throughout the drive. I was always in the backseat with the three boys and could see both Uncle Billy and Aunt Emmie. A few minutes later she would point at something and say, "Billy, what's that, Sug?" I never seen him look in the direction she was pointing as he replied, "I don't know, Mama?" After driving around for an hour or two, he'd head for home but always, always stopped at Krispy Kreme for a dozen of glazed donuts. Back home, everyone got a donut and a glass of milk. I stayed with them for eight or nine months and their routine was etched in stone. It was nice to have heat, and food and never hear cussing or arguments or being told how much I'm hated.

Uncle Billy

Aunt Emmie

After a while, Aunt Emmie insisted I go to school and it was at least twice the walk from her house to go to John Milledge School. I did go for a while but when it started getting really cold out and I still didn't have decent shoes or a coat. I only had a thin jacket and finally decided heck with this and I went back home. During this same time, I stayed at Aunt Emmie's, Dale had also left home and stayed with her friend Linda Richardson. Linda was married with a family and also lived in the project. Not sure how long Dale lived with them or when she came back home. When I entered the house back home, Mama never asked where I had been for almost a year. She just said, "It's yo turn to do the dishes."

That's about what Mama said to each one of us when we returned. Jewel said Mama said the same thing to her after she returned from staying with Aunt Erma. (Erma was Daddy's sister-in-law, married to his brother David. But they picked up and moved to Indiana.)

I felt bad that we all deserted Joyce. I never gave it a thought before I walked out that day to leave home. She was so little and so young and left there to fend for herself with two drunks! A nine-year-old alone shouldn't have to try to figure out how to get something to eat, how to stay warm, how to ward off half drunken strange men and get them out of the house and how to stay out of mama's wrath when mama did sober up. Joyce was used to having sisters to depend on, to follow and who made her feel safe. It never occurred to me she would have to go to that bathroom alone at night LOL; bless her heart. That was scary for me too and I had her to drag in there with me! She later told me she was scared all the time. I can only imagine. The unit on Broad Street seemed so big to us since we had moved there from that little shotgun house and it was at least twice that size.

So, with Mama and Daddy passed out drunk, especially if the electric was turned off, she must've felt like she was living in a horror film. I wish she had gone to Granny's or to Aunt Shirley's but she stayed… alone. She said she's had a fear of dying in her sleep most of her life and she doesn't know what that stems from or exactly when it started. But as long as she can re-member when she lays down to go to sleep at night, she is afraid she will die in her sleep. Not just a little fearful, I'm talking an overwhelming dreadful fear. (I found out later, when Joyce was fourteen years old, she had moved to Texas with a family without Mama knowing or caring where she was! I guess Daddy didn't know or care either. That happened after she was the only one of us left at home.)

Upon arriving back home from Aunt Emmie's, I found out the Heights had moved away. The Hodges had moved away, the Williams had moved away also. We had new neighbors on both sides. In the Hodges place was a family named Morris, Dot and David and they had six kids. To the right downstairs, just below us, was David Morris's sister, Gloria, and her friend Faye. Gloria was married to a long-distance trucker and she and Faye had a real good time on his money while he was away. They both stayed in bra and panties, only, while at home, but I have to admit, it was very hot there in the summer. I guess they weren't use to not having air conditioning or maybe they came from up north, but either way they didn't like to put clothes on. They didn't live there any time though and soon my Aunt Shirley and Uncle Glynn moved into that unit with their five kids. But they didn't live there long either.

I also discovered my mama had a brand-new boy-friend named Otis Padgett. Where on God's green earth she met him is still a wonder. She never left the house, he lived in South Carolina and he didn't drink so Daddy didn't bring him in from Frank and Broad or Al's Place. I've always wondered how she could possibly have met him. Otis was in his sixties, short, fat, white haired and so ugly his face could stop a clock! He had a wattle just like a turkey hanging from his neck and his gut was so huge he had to sit with one knee east and the other knee west out of necessity. Over the next three years, he was a regular "visitor" at our house. When Mama was sober, he would show up, always coming up the back stairs and parking his old black car in the backyard. Mama would comb her shoulder length hair, always the same style, with sectioning off each side and the top from ear to ear. Starting from the end of one side section she would roll it around and around until the curl reached her head and she held it there with two bobby pins.

Then she'd do the other side the same way and then the top was curled around and down as she pushed it toward her face so that it stood up somewhat and pinned to one side. She combed the rest back into a ponytail and put on her least pissed up shorts out of the two pair she owned, a green pair and a pink pair. She also only owned a couple blouses and had to constantly locate all the buttons and sew them back on by hand after every conniption fit. As soon as she had got herself ready to go, she'd say, "We'll be back in a little while; we're going to SC to buy some eggs." None of us were ever allowed to go with them and hours later they returned.

Her hair wasn't quite as neat returning as it was when she left. They would have eggs, cheese, light bread, and syrup. Sometimes they'd bring in some hamburger meat and get this now; Otis would open up the butcher's wrapping paper, never washing his hands, he would scoop him up a handful of hamburger meat, add a ton of salt and pepper to it and eat it raw! Mama never said a word about that to him. On the other hand, when we sat down to eat, we not only had to scrub our hands like we're fixing to perform surgery but we weren't allowed to reach into the light bread wrapper! SHE had to hand us a slice of bread because we were too contaminated to touch the inside of the wrapper. Sometimes they brought in a couple cans of Georgia Hash and rice and light bread. At times she'd have a can of hog brains to go with the eggs. Also, there were times he also got her some cinnamon rolls and milk, which was her favorite. Mama wasn't much of a cook; in fact, almost everything came from a can. She could make beans, rice, and boiled cabbage. Daddy made better cornbread patties than she did and she wouldn't know how to even begin to make a pie or cookies. She couldn't even make good tea, so she mostly fixed Kool-Aid. We girls had to teach ourselves to cook for the most part after were married. Otis always had to buy her some liquor and the electric was turned back on and there was kerosene for the three-burner stove and I assume he paid our rent that month. It would take another two to three months for the electric bill to get behind enough for it to be turned off again, so we were set for a while. Except that she then got drunk by the next day or two and by the time she sobered up the electric would be back off and it would start all over again with Otis. There was even a couple times when Mama and Otis came back they actually had bought some school paper. And if they made the mistake of buying it in the form of a composition book, we'd make us up an "Opinion" book instead of using it for school, which was a whole lot more fun!

Not too long before Jewel was released from the training school Otis and Mama and Dale and Joyce and I all went in Otis's car to Atlanta to see Jewel. It had been over a year since we had seen her and she was so happy to have visitors and see her family. She seemed nicer and more clam than I remembered her. Of course, all prisoners are probably nice to their visitors. We all sat outside in the back of the Training School grounds. They had four sided benches built surrounding trees to sit on and we were sitting around one tree when Dale was attack by bees. She being scared and jerking all around to avoid being stung, fell backwards into a deep hole that was between the benches and the tree trunk. Joyce was yelling, "Dale fell in a hole! Mama, Dale fell in a hole!" Mama and Otis had went inside to sign Jewel out for visitation and didn't see what happed to Dale but could hear Joyce and me yelling at them as they made their way back toward us. Mama said, "Where's Dale?" Joyce and I both at the same time saying, "We towed ya, she fell in a dang hole!!!!" Otis and Mama had to reach way down and take Dale's hands to get her out! It was a very deep hole but she got away from them bees! It was very sad saying good-bye to Jewel and it was obvious from her expression she was gonna cry once we left. I felt so sorry for her, we all did. And, "Oh yeah Jewel, here's our new address!"

Jewel was finally released from the Atlanta Training School and came home. She was almost never home though. She was like a bird outta the cage she was! But it was her turn with dishes!

This next part I probably shouldn't tell but it happened and it's something I have never been able to forget because it certainly isn't something a child should have to even overhear, let alone be told!

Joyce and I came home from running the streets as usual, but it was so hot that day we couldn't bear it anymore so we decided to go home. Well, evidently Daddy and Vincent Griffith couldn't bear to roof in the heat that day either. When we got upstairs and entered the living room, Daddy was standing there looking out the window toward the backyard. He was just standing there with his back to us. One of us asked, "Hey, Daddy, wut you doing home?" He turned around and just started to rant and rage. He said, "I came home because we couldn't work out there in this heat. I looked around for yo Mama and when I looked in our bedroom, there was her and Otis FUCKING!" (I had never heard that word come outta my daddy's mouth before and it was shocking to me! Back then that word was never used or heard period, even by the lowest of the low class.) He went on, "When I swung that door open and Otis seen me, he jumped off yo mama and he had the biggest hard on! His dick was so big and so hard! The sweat was just pouring off him and her both! He grabbed his britches and took off outta here and down the backstairs. You could tell he was surprised to see me home, yeah, yeah, I bet they BOTH was surprised to see me! But his dick was so big and so hard!" He kept saying that and I wondered where Mama was now and why he would say that to his own little kids. Even as young as we were, we knew that's not something that should be said in front of one's kids and it bothers me to this day that he did that. I mean, heck, we all knew what was going on with Otis and so did he! He knew Otis and Mama left the house and came home with food and the electric bill paid! He certainly knew Otis wasn't doing that because he was just a charitable person! Hell, Tebbie Stewart still came around too! The kin folks knew, the neighbors knew, we kids knew and we knew that he knew! It had been going on our entire lives, was no secret, so why the jealousy fit? I reckon because he seen it with his own eyes or because it was happening in their bed. Who knows? But he never brought it up again after that day and he never apologized to us kids for what he said to us.

Another day upon coming home I found Otis in Mama's bedroom and she was passed out cold! She was lying on her side with her back to Otis and he had all four fingers up inside her green shorts! I hollered, "Wut the hell are you doing?" He turned around looking at me with a big grin on his face and said, "I was trying to wake yo Mama up." I said, "I KNOW wut you were doing and you better leave!" He kept laughing as he made his way out the back door. Years later Jewel told me she came home late one night while we lived on Broad Street and Mama and Daddy were both passed out in the bed. She came up the backstairs because the backdoor was almost always unlocked and as she passed through the living room she heard some weird noises coming from Mama and Daddy's bedroom. She went over and looked inside and there was James H.'s daddy on top of Mama. She began to beat on his back and telling him to get out. He jumped up but she wouldn't stop hitting him so he couldn't get his clothes. He said let me get my clothes and she said hell no, you're leaving just like you are. She chased him down the steps and he had nothing on but a pair of socks! He had to go home naked! She went back into the bedroom and searched his pants pockets and took what little money he had, which was just had a couple dollars and a little change. Don't know if he ever came back for his pants and shoes. There have been others I could name here too but because they were married to kin folks at the time, I'll keep that to myself.

We were subjected to things little kids should never have to witness. And because of Mama's loose morals and Daddy bringing men into our house, we ALL had a reputation. But we girls were not whores!!!! We ran the streets looking for food but we never slept with someone period let alone so we could eat. We never allowed any of those men to touch us and we didn't have boyfriends we slept with. People just assumed what was going on and they didn't have a clue. It's too bad someone somewhere didn't care enough about us to have us removed and placed in a children's home permanently. But in their defense, it wasn't easy to get someone's kids taken away from them. Had folks back then had the videoing capabilities as we have today, they could've made a case against Mama and Daddy rather than he said, she said, scenario it would've been in a courtroom back then.

I remember a time when I first came back from Aunt Emmie's house and Otis was sitting at our kitchen table. I was just beginning to have boobies, which looked more like swollen nipples through my clothes. Otis called me over and when I went over to see what he wanted he pinched my nipple. I tried to slap his face, which really didn't make contact because he jerked his head back so I used my other hand to slap him just as Mama came back into the kitchen. She seen me trying to slap him and started jumping all over me. I told her what he had done and she said, "I don't give a damn; you say you're sorry right now!" I turned and walked away without saying anything. But I sure got the message that my own Mama wouldn't defend me against a dirty old man. Just when I thought I couldn't think any less of her, I shocked myself with how much lower my opinion of her could go.

There were signs... besides Mama coming straight out telling us and screaming at us that she hates us and wishes we were never born she showed it in many other ways also. There was a tree in our backyard that had a rope tied to a branch way up high and we could swing from the rope to the ground if we held our legs up. Otis had his car parked under that tree and Joyce went to swing from the rope and the long silver hood ornament went into her thigh. She swung right into it so it made a very deep and large hole in her leg. The meat was falling out, it was pitiful and Mama did nothing. She has a horrible scar there to this day because it was taken care of. Had it been taken care of correctly, I'm sure the scar would be much less than it is. Dale and I both, at different times, cut our big toe wide open by walking through the water that rushes toward the sewers in the curbs after it rained. Busted glass or metal or whatever, we never could tell exactly what cut us.

Dale said she remembers Mama pouring kerosene over her cut, her usual solution to everything. But she wouldn't even look at my toe when I cut it. We certainly didn't own any antiseptics or Band-Aids or bandages of any kind. I just had to find a rag and tried to tie it onto my foot as it bled and bled. Then there was the time I was trying to push the lenses outta a pair of sunglasses. I had found the glasses somewhere and one lens was missing already. I wanted the glasses to look like regular glasses so I tried to push out the other lens with my left thumb. The lens broke and cut a big spiral shaped cut into my thumb. It wouldn't stop bleeding and it hurt so much. The skin had a piece of meat attached to it and had flopped down. I showed Mama since she just happened to be sober and her only response was, "I bet 'ya won't do that again." I tried to fold the flop back to my thumb and hold it close by tying a strip of some rag on it. When it finally healed, I realized the flesh inside was folded or something because it has never been right since. To this day, if I press down on anything with my left thumb as I rotate it side to side, it is extremely painful. Mama just never cared to be bothered with any of our problems or wounds. She really never had any natural affection or concern for her kids. There was never any antiseptic or aspirins or anything of the kind there. The closest thing would be rubbing alcohol but Mama and Daddy drank that up. We were never taken to a dentist or a doctor, ever.

We all took turns doing the dishes. Dale hated that the most; she would sell you her soul if you'd do them for her! Anything she owned would be yours if you took her turn. We never had regular dishwashing detergent. We had a bar of soap, that's it. They would buy, or maybe Otis would buy a bag of those cheap Bouquet bars, maybe six bars in a bag. We had to first heat some water on the kerosene stove if we had kerosene, on the potbellied stove if we didn't have the kerosene. In the summertime of course we couldn't fire up a potbellied stove anyhow so we'd have to wait until we had kerosene. But to wash dishes we had to take a knife and shave the bar of soap into the hot water we poured in the sink. Trying to clean dishes like that was crazy, especially if they were greasy. If Mama came across ANY that wasn't clean to her specifications, which meant spotless, she would make us do them ALL over again. Every last one! She would cuss us and threaten us if they weren't done right. She threw them, broke the coffee cups, plates, mason jars, jelly glasses etc. ALL of our coffee cups had the handles missing. Plates had cracks in 'em; jelly jars had chips in the glass that you'd have to be mighty careful not to cut yourself on. She would actually stomp the boilers (what we called pots). Then when she needed a boiler to cook something in, she'd take a hammer and beat it back into shape. The bottoms always wobbled from being so lumpy and when they sat on the kerosene burner, they would drip and make a spit sizzle noise.

Once in a blue moon Mama would be in a good mood but there were prerequisites that had to be met. A, she had to be over her hangover. B, she had to have had something to eat that she liked. C, she had something sweet to eat. And D, she wasn't ready to get drunk again. That's the times she would rake. She loved putting rake marks in the dirt! The grass in our backyard was very sparse and mostly a powdery sand over red dirt and she would rake, even though there wasn't anything to rake up as in leaves and such. She just liked drawing a line in the sand with a rake and I know she thought it made her look like a good housekeeper to the neighbors. It really didn't but she thought it did.

Toilet paper at our house usually was torn sheets of newspapers and Daddy always managed to get a hold of someone's phone book that they were throwing out. And those bars of soap were also what we had to brush our teeth and wash our clothes with on a scrub board in the tub. If we had soap powders we had no bar soap, if we had bar soap, the usual, we had no soap powders. Then we had to take the clothes down the back steps to the backyard to hang them out. On Broad St we did have bottom sheets on our beds that they acquired somewhere and Mama would at times take the bed sheets and hang them on the line outside to dry without them being washed. Big ole yellowish circles on 'em all over one overlapping the other. She said she hung them outside to try and embarrass us into not wetting our beds. (What about her and Daddy pissing all over their bed? At least ours wasn't after drinking wine, paint thinner or camp heat!) I remember when she used to beat us for wetting the beds. She never wet the bed as a child and she accused us of being too lazy to get up and sit on the slop jar! Daddy did wet the bed as a child and he knew what it was like to have to go through that. To always stink and have a wet bed, especially in the winter time. Who in their right minds would pee in their bed deliberately? He told her, "Please don't whoop 'em for that, they can't help it." She said, "Well I've tried beating it out of 'em but it ain't done one bit of good, they're all lazy sum bitches!" Then when he asked her not to cuss us, she'd cuss him. But if ya wanna talk about embarrassing, Daddy hanging his underwear in the window takes the cake! He had a giant pair of lady's baby doll pajama bottoms they got from some place. Most likely was in a box of clothes someone gave us. They looked like they were extra-extra-large, like made for a 350 lb. woman. They were white (or use to be) with whole large strawberries printed on them all over and tiny gathers around the elastic on each leg. That was Daddy's only underwear and at night when he went to bed, he'd hang them in the window above their bed to air out. (That window faced the backyard!) Then the next night he'd turn them inside out and hang them in the window so they'd be fresh as a daisy the next day. Night after night after night he hung them in the window, inside out then right side out, then inside out, then right side out. He would wear his cutoffs while he aired out the underwear. His cutoffs were what he called an old pair of pants he cut the legs off to make shorts. He always changed into them every evening when he came in and aired his strawberry drawers in the window. Of course, I'm speaking of his routine when he was sober.

One day I came home from somewhere, not sure where I had been or how long I was out but there must've been one rip-roaring fight with them because there was a stove wedged on the front stairs. It was wedged diagonally from one wall to the other wall about half way down. We had to climb over it to go upstairs. After it was there for a couple days I went to Granny's house and spent a couple nights and when I came home the stove was gone. I never knew what happened for sure but I think I know. They never had the gas turned on, heck they couldn't keep the electric on half the time let alone gas too. That's why we had to heat the water on the kerosene stove. The kitchen stove was gas and the three-burner kerosene stove sat on top of the gas stove. Mama probably was raising hell at Daddy about not being able to have an oven or cook with gas and the arguing escalated until he grabbed the stove and threw it down the steps. I figure this went down like that because our kerosene stove then sat on a different piece of furniture and it was much higher up which made it even harder to cook. We could hardly see over the edge of the pots then. (A couple years later we would have to cook on an iron turned upside down and propped up with books and such, then sat a frying pan on the iron. I'm telling ya, life was an adventure!)

We all stayed gone from home as much as possible and Joyce and I still roamed the streets of Augusta. A person could get into the movie theater for ten bottle caps so we'd go to many stores and drink machines in search for them. Judy had told me once that if we ever ran across any kids that went to Martha Lester School or from Frog Hollow, they would be our enemies. Frog Hollow was the other side of Augusta. She didn't say why, just said to stay clear of them. I believed every word she said without question so the next time we went on an Augusta Excursion, I informed Joyce if we meet any kids while out and about who say they go to Martha Lester or they're from Frog Hollow then we would run as fast as we could away from them. She said okay because she believed every word I said without question.

We heard somewhere that Betty Joyce Rabin from up the street had a water head brother and we were just uncouth and dumb enough to go up there and ask her. After the first time asking someone that, you'd think we wouldn't have that mush nerve! But she said she did indeed have a water head brother and we could see him. She took us into their front room where there was a crib against the wall. Sho'nuff there was a water head boy in it. Betty Joyce said his name was "shit-ass" and he was nine years old. He looked to be about three years old and I wondered why, if he was nine, he couldn't speak. He was extremely thin and he kept putting his foot in his mouth and making grunting noises. He seemed so happy to be seeing someone near him. It was obvious he was very bored and lonely since he couldn't get up. He spent his every waking moment in that crib and I wished we had never asked to see him since it was so heart wrenching.

Joyce and I decided to pay the Copeland's a visit one day while we were out excursionating (my word, LOL) since we were close by their house. We knew they were kinfolk but didn't know how, back them anyway. Uncle Ed and Aunt Louise and Aunt Bertha was Mama Hall's people which made them Mama's people which made them our people as near as we could figure. But we didn't know them at all, just knew of them. So, we knock on the door and told them we were Lorraine's kids. They were kind and hospitable and asked how our Mama was doing. (We almost cracked up!) But to make a long story short we said, "She's finer than frog's hair." They had just got up from the dining room table and I hadn't seen that much food except in the school cafeteria! It was a big table and slap full of bowls and platters and plates filled with cooked groceries! They placed a large linen tablecloth over everything. I asked why they were covering their food like that. Aunt Louise said that was dinner and were leaving it out for supper. Joyce and I both jerked our heads toward each other and I'm sure our eyes said it all! Like in a cartoon when their eyes bug out! Lawd, it was hard not to ask for something to eat! They all moseyed out to the front porch to sit so we talked for a spell and then we left. We said to one another, "Can you believe they had that much food? AND they eat like that more than once a day? It ain't even Sunday"! "And "Yeah, I bet ya they even cooked a big breakfast too!" "Yeah, they're so lucky!" We never stopped in again, that was just too hard to see! LOL. We told Mama all about it and of course she got her nose all twisted and wanted to know exactly what we told them about her and Daddy. I wish we would've answered, "We told them yaw was away on your yacht for the week!"

I stopped in to see Becky Weeks once, the only time I was ever in her house. A man who lived across the street from us, Jimmy Odom, had called me over and asked me if I would go to Becky's house and ask her if she would go off with him. He was married but I thought what the heck, that's up to her to care about that or not. When I got there Becky's Mama who was on her way out said to go on in, she's in there. So, I yelled for Becky and Becky answered, "I'm in here, come on back." So, I did and she was in the tub surrounded with all her dirty clothes in the tub with her! I said to her, "You bathe with your clothes?" She said, "Uh-huh, it's a lot easier than leaning over the tub." The water was almost black! She was probably only fourteen or fifteen years old at that time. I thought that was so funny. So, I told her Jimmy had said and she looked like she was thinking about it but didn't answer and I didn't want to watch her wash her clothes naked so I left.

Becky came to our house looking for Dale who was the same age as her. Not that Dale hung around her that much. I was sitting on the porch and I told her Dale wasn't home. Becky asked me if I'd walk downtown with her to go to the movies, she'd pay my way in and buy me something to eat. Well, she didn't have to ask me twice! That's a pretty long walk but dinner and a movie was worth every step! So, we get to the Imperial Theater and right next door was Snappy Hamburgers, and they had a special on, a dozen burgers for one dollar. Getting in the movies only cost like 15 cents or a quarter. I assumed Becky was buying me some popcorn and a coke or a hotdog and a coke but instead she bought the dozen burgers, ONE order of fries and ONE coke. We go sat down in the theater and she hands me ONE burger! ONE! They are a 3"by 3" burger, like on a Hawaiian King Dinner roll. She drank the coke and ate the fries and ate all the rest of the burgers. Eleven, ELEVEN BURGERS! I think I glared at her more than the movie for the next two hours!

Poor Becky came upstairs to our house one day and we happen to be sitting at the table eating dinner. (Due to Mama being sober.) The table was a fairly long table and the one end was pushed against the far wall and Mama always sat on the other end which was in the middle of the kitchen and we kids sat on either side. I don't remember how many of us were home and at the table but we were eating Butterbeans and fried cornbread patties. Becky walked up right beside Mama and leaned over to pick up one of the cornbread patties. Mama jumped up, grabbed her plate of food, and threw it against the opposite wall! There was Butterbeans all over the place and sliding down the wall. She threw a cup too that had some onion wedges in it and the cup stuck into the wall, while she was yelling and cussing.

Mama said, "Who in the hell do you think you are coming in here and leaning over my G**Damn plate! Ain't no damn body gonna touch my G**Damn food! I don't allow my own damn young'uns to lean over my food, and you damn shore ain't!!!! Becky couldn't have looked more shocked if she had stuck her finger in a light socket with both feet in water! Meanwhile Mama stomped into the living room and grabbed the rabbit ears on the TV and twists them until they looked like the world's largest Bobby Pins! Becky was tall and solid but must have weighed 300 pounds or close to it, and when she took off down the front steps it sounded like

a herd of elephants at full speed ahead! She didn't come around again for the longest time.

Mama never cared whose feelings she hurt! She would have told President Kennedy to kiss her royal behind if he made her mad, and if he wasn't good looking!

Fourth of July in the south was also known as Fantastic Day. Kids would dress up in a funny costume and walk around the neighborhoods, while the adults sit out on their porches and enjoyed laughing at them. Whoever chose to have that ritual during the hottest time of year, Dog Days, I don't know because it was certainly too hot to be dressing up in a costume. Joyce and I did it, not sure if our sisters ever did. We would fold a bed pillow over a belt and then strapped on the belt with the folded pillow resting on our behind. Then put on a pair of Daddy's pants over it and roll up the legs of the britches. Or if we could find a big enough dress, we'd use that instead. We pretty much did it as the kids in the picture below. We didn't have masks, just drew on big eyebrows and mustache. It was so hot with all that clothing on but it made people laugh and we certainly enjoyed doing it.

When I was in the fourth grade and classes resumed after Christmas vacation, the teacher said we're gonna start with the first row and first desk and each student can stand up and tell us what you each received for Christmas. The first kid stood up and named off a bunch of stuff and then the next and the next. Row after row each kid beaming with pride as they told of all their gifts. I knew it was coming to my turn and I wasn't about to stand up and say I received nothing… not even a Christmas dinner! So, I begin to think of everything I was gonna say. By the time it got to me I had a list in my mind, and so I stood up and named off all the stuff I had wished for. The very first thing I named off was a Tiny Tear Doll. I had seen the commercial on TV and I wanted that doll so badly that my hurter hurt! Of course, I never got it. Based on my clothing, shoes, no lunch money or lunch and it being obvious I didn't even bathe very often, I'm sure the teacher didn't believe a word of it, and probably the kids didn't either.

But I hope that taught her a lesson, to not do that to kids. No matter what some kids received, there would always be kids who got better or more and some would certainly feel worse and some would feel prideful. It just goes to show not all teachers have common sense. To this day when I hear the song, "Shake Me I Rattle, Squeeze Me I Cry," which is about a woman who wanted a doll she saw in the store window when she was little but didn't have enough money. Later she sees a little girl looking longingly through a toy shop window at an identical doll. So, the woman buys the doll and gives it to the little girl. (I can see myself doing that.) But the song brings up those feelings I had back when I wanted that Tiny Tear doll.

I only remember getting free school lunches for a couple years. Good Lawd their food was good! To sit in class and smell the food being prepared all morning was heaven, knowing I would be getting some. I didn't play hooky nearly as much for those couple years. We left for school on an empty stomach and would have no supper at home if Mama was drunk, so the only food we would get is the school lunch. The years we didn't get a free lunch was because Mama refused to do all that paperwork to apply. She would've had to fill out a form for each child stating the parent's names, address, income, employer's name and address and phone number, how many people were in the family, how much the rent was, child's name, age, birth date, which school the child attended, etc. I don't know what all they asked but it was a pretty long form. She didn't know anything about copy paper or copy machines and wasn't about to fill all that out for each kid, so we did without. I asked my teachers during those years without lunch could I please remain at my desk in the classroom. I told them I would lay my head on the desk and take a nap but every time I was told no. I must go to the lunchroom and sit there because kids aren't allowed to be in the classroom without supervision since there had been kids who stole from the coatroom. It was bad enough to be that hungry but to be forced to watch other kids eat was just plain cruel, so those years we played hooky a LOT! I remember the day I took a sandwich to school. I was ten years old and I was so proud that the other kids would see I had something to eat too! I had discovered a couple ends of the white bread left in the wrapper, we called light bread. The only thing I could find to put on it was a small amount of dark Karo syrup. I remember holding that bottle upside down for the longest time while a very thin thread of syrup came out onto one of the bread ends. I made a round and round design on the bread until no more would come out. I wish I had had enough sense to place the 'sandwich' back into the plastic bread bag but I didn't. I looked around for something to put it in and found a brown paper grocery bag. The size the store gave you if you bought a loaf of bread maybe. It wasn't gigantic but it was certainly three times the size of a lunch bag. I put the 'sandwich' inside and rolled the top of the bag all the way down and carried it to school. Lunchtime came and I proudly opened my bag and pulled out my sandwich. Stupid me opened the sandwich right in front of everyone and what little bit of syrup was on it had seeped inside the bread and was all dried up. I could barely see the swirls the syrup had made and I close it back up and began to eat it. Some of the kids were laughing and saying, "EWW, EWW, you gonna eat that?" I didn't know whether to be proud I had a lunch or embarrassed I had a lunch; I was totally confused at that point! I didn't have a drink but got a drink of water in the hall fountain on the way back to class.

When school first started in the fall each year, I can remember sitting at my desk and looking around and it seemed like just about all the little girls had on new clothes. They all wore socks and shiny pat and leather black or white shoes, or Bobbie socks and Saddle shoes or sneakers. I knew I stood out like a sore thumb in my clothes that were always too big or too little depending on who use to own them. I had a pair of yellow pointed toed slip-on shoes one year that I believe use to be Jewel's or Judy's. They had a little square flat heel on the bottom but the heels had worn almost completely away. There were tiny nails sticking up inside the shoes and hurting my feet so I pulled the nails out! The heels fell off then and when I walked in them, I could feel a slight rocking backwards to the shoes with every step. By the time I got home from school, there were holes that went all the way through where the heels use to be. So, I folded newspaper and made a lining to cover the holes. I soon realized I had to do that every day because the newspaper didn't hold up well walking on roads and sidewalks and even more so if it rained. The shoes flopped a little because they were also too big for me but I wore them all that year. I could feel the cold from the ground right through the shoes all winter. So, I would look at the shoes and socks the other girls wore and I wanted some of those white socks with the lace edge and the shiny black pat and leather shoes so bad… I thought how lucky those girls were. I remember while looking at some girl's shoes several desks ahead and one row over, how I could see the bottom of their shoes when she held her feet a certain way. Then I remembered what the bottom of my shoes looked like with the holes and the newspaper showing through, so I made a conscious effort to never cross my feet that way so the kids behind me couldn't see the bottoms of my shoes. I will never forget those damn yellow shoes.

In the fifth and sixth grades I mostly either played hooky or went in and immediately laid my head on my desk and went to sleep. The loud bell woke me up for recess, lunch time the teacher woke me to sit and watch the other kids eat and the bell woke me again at three o'clock to leave. The reason being is, right at the beginning of the school year and class in session the teacher would say, "Class, take out your Arithmetic books." She then would tell us which problems to work. I raised my hand and once I was finally acknowledged I would tell her I have no paper. She would say, "Would someone give Gloria a piece of paper?" Usually someone would hand me a sheet of paper. Then I raised my hand again… finally she'd ask again what I wanted. "I don't have a pencil." "Would someone loan Gloria a pencil?" Usually someone did. Then it was take out the spelling books, same problem, I have no paper. After three or four times of others handing me paper, no one was offering anymore. The teacher didn't seem to notice whether someone gave me paper or not after the first couple times. Or maybe she was as tired of it as the other students seemed to be. Either way, I stopped telling her and just laid my head down and went to sleep. She didn't say a word about it so I assumed she didn't care that I slept through class. So, after day one of school, I simply went to class and went straight to sleep. The only times I participated was when I could bring my own notebook paper, which was rarely. There was a boy who sat in the back of the classroom in my sixth grade who was extremely tall for his age or was way older than the rest of us, His name was Clifford P. (I know his last name but not gonna say here.) but he just decided to light up a cigarette and smoke it right there in class. I was waiting to see what the teacher was gonna do but I was thinking, "Dang, he's cool!" She sent him to the principal's office. He probably went out the door instead and left the building. That was just a funny memory that popped into my head.

When I returned home from living with my Aunt Emmie, Judy was working as a server in a café or restaurant at Fort Gordon Army base. She took the bus there and back every day. Poor Judy, she couldn't have anything for us. She bought cigarettes at the BX for $2.00 a carton instead of the $2.50 a carton at the stores. So, she'd buy a carton of Winston and hide them in the top of our bedroom closet. We'd always find them and take a pack! Boy, she'd be fighting mad! Literally! She'd hurt ya over her stuff. She had bought herself an orange flared dress and crinoline and I discovered it in the closet while she was at work. So, I put them on and was prancing up and down the sidewalk when she came home! OMG, she threatened to rip them off me if I didn't take them off immediately. She was four years older than me and of course I was scared of her because, like Mama, she showed no mercy when she lit into ya! I did take them off and promised to leave her stuff alone but she glared at me with a sneer that only Judy could produce for hours on end. Every time I looked her way, she was staring at me like she wanted to slit my throat!

We all smoked at a very young age, everyone smoked back them. It was the cool thing to do and almost every commercial on TV was a cigarette commercial. I actually started smoking in the fifth grade and since the stores sold cigarettes to kids, and I could babysit for a couple dollars, I'd buy a pack for 25 cents and spent the rest on RC Colas, Moon Pies, candy, hamburger, etc. Daddy would, per Mama's instructions, occasionally buy one pack of cigarettes and divide them up with Dale and Judy and Jewel and I. We each got five cigarettes. Daddy finally came home with a cigarette rolling machine and would buy a pack of Bugle for 10 cents and we had to roll our own. We didn't like them but it was something to smoke. So, the days we did go to school, we'd go into the girl's bathroom and light one up. We'd be in a stall and pass the cigarette back and forth and the fire on the end would get two inches long! They had "patrol" girls in the restroom to run girls out who wanted to linger. Well, of course, we wanted to linger, we were smoking! And on top of that, it was too cold to be outside where all the other kids would be walking around and around the school yard, circling the building until the bell rang to come in.

We didn't have warm clothes, coats, and socks like most of them had, but they didn't have cigarettes like we had. I'm sure we reeked of cigarette smoke when we did enter our classroom. (Of course, most of the teachers smelled like smoke also so they may not have noticed it on us as much.) There was this one patrol girl, I don't remember her name, just that she was tall and had brown hair, who obviously thought she was the restroom sheriff and she didn't like us Palmer girls at all. She was always trying to run us out of there and we were just as determined to stay in there and out of the cold until that bell rang. She got into an argument with Dale and threatened to beat Dale up after school. After school, she was nowhere around so we went on home. The following day, Dale wasn't in school, she either didn't feel good or played hooky I can't recall which, but I had gone to school and was in the restroom when I overheard Miss Sheriff of the restroom telling others that Dale wasn't in school that day because she did indeed beat Dale up after school the day before. When I got home, I told Dale what was being said in the restroom. The following day Dale was never so excited to go to school as she was that day! We walked into the girl's restroom and there stood Miss high and mighty wearing her white shoulder strap belt with a large silver badge pinned at chest level and ordering girls around as usual. Dale walks straight up to her, drops her purse to the floor and knocked the cold living hell out of her. The fight was on! They went around and around and when it was over the girl had three or four very deep scratches the entire length of her face on one side. It was horrible looking.

We went on to class and a within an hour or two we were called into the principal's office. The patrol girl and her parents were there also. Her parents were threatening to sue because they said she would need cosmetic surgery to fix her face. I assume the principal assured them we weren't the type of family that could be sued. (What could they get from the Palmer family???) But as of that day Dale was suspended from school and we both left and headed home clicking our heels and doing somersaults all the way (JK), NO MORE SCHOOL! YAY! We done learned all we needed to anyways! Although we felt bad for the girl who would most likely have those facial scars for the rest of her life, we thought she should've brought more than her face to a cat fight. That was probably the only time Mama was proud of one of her kids… Dale and I were both in the sixth grade and Joyce was in the fourth, none of us ever went back. Elizabeth B Hamilton and Miss Savage came only once after that. We came in the house just as Mama was saying, "Git the hell outta my house before I stomp the hell outta both of ya! And don't jew ever come back round here!" Not sure what they said to get Mama that riled up but it must've been some sort of a threat to her. I didn't know Liz B Hamilton and old lady Savage could move so fast. The school board didn't seem to care; at least they never bothered with us again after that.

We slept most of the days away and hung out on the front porch at night. Becky Weeks who lived up the street on the other side, in a real house came down and hung out with us a lot. The Laney's who lived two porches up had six kids and I became best friends with Delvia Laney. We both liked the same boy, Don Cook, and he was her boyfriend first then mine. Then he was just a memory to us both and although you'd think that would've made Delvia and me enemies, it didn't. Our friendship continues to this day. We even said we'd name our daughters after one another. She has a beautiful daughter now and she kept her word and named her Gloria. I had three sons and my husband wouldn't let me name one Delvia. I'll admit, it's a little too feminine for a boy. Delvia was taller than me and blond and very pretty.

Her older sister, Linda, was also blonde and gorgeous and always chewing gum which made a popping noise when she chewed. (I tried for years to do that but could never master it.) Delvia's other older sister, Verdice, was a heavy set girl with a beautiful face. She was way ahead of her time, having the heavy black drawn on eyebrows which is very popular with the models and stars today and she was very good at doing her makeup. Joyce or I would see Verdice coming up the walk and would beg her to sing for us. She had a beautiful soft voice and we loved it when she'd agree to sing. She'd sat on the steps and sang the song "Patches." I learned the lyrics from listening to her so many times and I still remember them. Mrs. Laney was the sweetest lady ever and I envied Delvia and her siblings for their awesome mom.

When it got so late at night that all the neighbor kids had gone home and the porch became boring, Joyce and I would lay across the bed upstairs looking out the window. We'd count how many "POPEYES" we spotted. (That's cars passing by with only one working taillight.) Traffic got lighter and lighter as the night got later and later. We poked holes in the screen window to push our cigarette butts through which fell on the ground below. We lay there and talk and laugh and just being silly until we could see dawn breaking and then we'd go to sleep.

Between Jewel, Judy, and Dale, they kept a supply of makeup, hairspray, and bobby pins on the dresser in the other bedroom and Joyce and I put it to good use! After teasing our hair we'd create a seductive movie star style. Pinning back just one side while brushing the top toward the other side, up high then coming down over the one side of our faces almost covering one eye then spraying it till it could stop a bullet. We'd put on makeup and always, always added two big black beauty marks with the twist of an eyebrow pencil. We placed one beauty mark high on the cheekbone just below the right eye, and the other just below the left corner of our mouth.

This is exactly like the Mascara we used on our eyelashes. We would spit in the little tray where the brush sits, then wet the brush with the spit and rub it into the black mascara. We all used the same one. (Gross huh?)

With the bobby pins we made dangle earrings by feeding three bobby pins into the bottom of one bobby pin, and then we clipped the single one on our earlobes. We would then put on a flared skirt and tuck one side up under our underwear so that one leg is exposed from the thigh down, (Just like the stars on TV!) We then took our hairbrush microphone into the big bedroom and the show began. I'd go in the closet while Joyce stood facing the beds (Our make-believe audience.) and say something like, "And now introducing the fabulous and beautiful Gloria Palmer! Then she'd applaud too loud and too long as I came from the closet and she'd hand me the microphone, I mean hairbrush. (I'd twirled around just like Loretta Young did when making her appearance on her TV show.) Then I'd start in with the song "Sad Movies Always Makes Me Cry." Afterwards, Joyce applauded again and darted into the closet and I'd introduce her to our pretend audience, "And now for your listening pleasure tonight, want you welcome the talented and lovely, one and only Joyce Palmer!" She'd come bounding out of the closet, taking the hairbrush while saying, "Thank you, thank you." She'd put her one leg forward that had the skirt hiked up so that it was front and center. She began to sing, "Patches"!!!!!! I'd think or sometimes even say, "Shoot, I was gonna do that song next!" And she would say the same thing on my next song. We did this back and forth, taking turns singing for several hours.

"Bye-Bye Love"

"Pretty Blue Eyes"

"Heartaches By the Number"

"Where The Boys Are"

"Lipstick on Your Collar"

"I've Told Every Little Star"

"It Keeps Right on A Hurtin'"

"A Thousand Stars in the Sky"

"I'm Gonna Knock on Your Door"

"I'm Sorry"

"Send Me the Pillow That You Dream On"

"Will You Still Love Me Tomorrow"

Many times, Lil' Genia came up to sing with us and the three of us took turns. She didn't go for the makeup and beehive hairdos; maybe she knew Aunt Mae would hit the ceiling if she did. Also, she liked to do the gospel songs more, so then we sang,

"How Far Is Heaven"
"Jesus Paid It All"
"Just a Little Talk with Jesus"
"Wings of A Snow-White Dove"
"He Set Me Free"
"Tramp on the Street"
"The Man from Galilee"
"Take Up Your Cross and Follow Me"

What's funny is when we'd sing "The Man from Galilee," we'd add "Licka, Licka, Lee" to that line!

And what's sad, is out of all the years we sang with just a small hallway separating us from Mama and Daddy, who were sitting in the living room if they were sober, they never once, nary single time did they ever peep around the doorway to watch us. As much as Daddy loved to sing and play his guitar, he never encouraged us or mentioned he noticed we love to sing. When he sang, he never asked if we'd like to sing one with him or while he played the guitar for us. The Ed Palmer show was on and yaw need to just sit and listen. I cannot even imagine overhearing my little kids put on a pretend show and singing their little hearts out and I had zero interest in at least sneaking a peep at 'em. Like I said before, the side of our bed where we would be sitting faced the hall, so there's no way we wouldn't have spotted them had they came toward our bedroom. This broke my heart when I grew up and looked back on these memories, not that I would expect any different from Mama who hated music of any kind, but I expected more from Daddy. I remember asking Daddy to teach me how to play the guitar but he said no because, "You cannot teach someone to play by ear and I play by ear." Years later I discovered he taught his great niece to play the guitar. A couple times we have observed Mama singing, or more speaking the words, "Daddy Coon, Daddy Coon" while rotating her hips when she was half lit. That was the closest thing to music you'd hear outta her.

Mama honest to God thought she was beautiful. She told us so many times and also how beautiful her legs are. She made it perfectly clear, once we had boyfriends coming around, that those boys were more interested in her than us. She would sit in their laps and grab their junk whenever she could. We girls never heard a compliment or even a hint at a compliment from Mama. Never heard her brag even a little on one of us or even so much as telling one of us we did a good job on something. She made it clear she was the star of this show.

Neither Mama nor Daddy has ever said, "I love you" to any of us as far as I know. I know I've never heard that from either of them. The closest thing to it was after I was grown and moved out of state, Daddy would write me a letter and sign it, "Love in Christ."

That's the same way one would sign a letter to an acquaintance I thought. But we did hear, "I hate you" quite often from Mama. At the dinner table Daddy would say grace, at least I think that's what he was doing. He bowed his head and mumbled something we couldn't hear. He never said it out loud or told us kids to bow our head as he said it or taught us to say grace before we eat. Mama never said grace in her life that I'm aware of.

One would think with Daddy going to Bible College for four years and being a preacher before, he would definitely be teaching his kids a lot about the word of God, but he didn't. What I remember him saying the most, throughout our entire childhood and had to be his favorite saying was, "Hope for the best but expect the worse." If I heard him say that once, I heard it hundreds of times. He was extremely negative about most everything. He constantly said things like, "You're damned if you do and damned if you don't!" and "We'll never have anything in this life!" and "Everyone's out to get ya!" and, "People just love to see ya fail or lose!" and, "You'll never get ahead in this life!" and "This world and one more and then the fireworks!" Whatever that meant. The only thing I can remember Daddy teaching me/us is telling us to never turn a corner, especially after dark, without first walking way out and then around. "Because he said you never know who might be just around the corner waiting to grab ya."

I mean there were times he'd walk around holding his cup of coffee and walking over to the window talking, sounded more like he was talking to himself than us. He'd say something like, "I'm tellin' ya, it's an awful thing to fall into the hands of the Living God!" But to sat us down and have a talk with us, nah, didn't happen. He mostly spoke of hell fire when he talked about the bible and how horrific hell will be. He almost never mentioned how wonderful Heaven will be or God's miracles. Sometimes he'd start crying and say if it wasn't for God's mercy he doesn't know where he'd be. But mostly he talked like that later on after we were grown.

By now, Jewel had met her dreamboat, married him, and moved out. She said she was sitting upstairs in that small bedroom at the dresser rolling her hair. Back then people could and would park their cars along the curb on Broad Street. There was an old car parked out front and this dude stopped to check it out. I assume he could see Jewel through the window because out of all four doors on that porch he knocked on our door. Jewel went down to the door, hair rollers and all, and there stood Lloyd Weeks. He asked her if she knew who owned the car out front because he was interested in buying it and fixing it up. She said she didn't know and he turned and walked away. About that time Becky Weeks came up and Jewel ask her if she knew who that guy was. Becky did indeed know him and said his name was Lloyd Weeks. (She wasn't kin to him despite the same last name.) Jewel said she fell in love with his muscles, she thought he was gorgeous and she decided then and there she was gonna marry him! She asked Becky to get her a date with him and she did. The rest is history; they've been married sixty-two years now.

Dot Morris, next door, happened to come out on the front porch while some of us were out there too. She introduced herself and told us her husband David was a painter and she worked in one of the cotton mills. She was so pretty, very thick natural wavy black hair with a widow's peak yet had beautiful blue eyes. Her natural skin tone looked as though she had a tan and she didn't wear a speck of makeup and didn't need to. She had an infectious laugh although she was a take care of business type person. She didn't take too kindly to Daddy flirting with her and she put him in his place immediately. I thought that was so cool, and I gained a lot of respect for her. Eventually, we met all six of her kids as well as her husband, David. He was a tiny man, smaller than Dot, with black hair, dark eyes and although he had his natural teeth, they seemed too large for his mouth which he made a grinding noise with all the time. He got drunk most evenings after work but Dot didn't drink. Jerry was the oldest of the six, then Carl, then Gene, then Ricky, Janet, and Eddie. As soon as I laid eyes on Jerry who was three years older than me, I fell in love! He had the blackest hair and bluest eyes. When he smiled his eyes almost disappeared they were so squinty. He loved to wear taps on his black loafer shoes because he liked the sound when he walked. He called them cleats but they were taps he had only on the heels. He always wore black slacks and a white shirt. And as fate would have it, he was crazy about me too and we spent more and more time on the porch together. I believe I was twelve when I met Jerry and he was fifteen. Our dating consisted of sitting on the porch. He never invited me up to his house and I never invited him inside of mine. He didn't have any money, and no way to get any so we never walked to the movies downtown or to the What-A-Burger stand or to the drugstore for ice cream. It was just stealing a kiss on the front porch and talking. I cannot remember what we ever talked about since I never knew if he went to school or had already dropped out or if he dropped out sometime later and at what age. Or if he believed in God or where he moved to Broad Street from or any of the things I would think would've come up. I really didn't know much about him and he never ask me anything either. He only told me about a cousin he had named Billy Rubin who he bragged and bragged about. Obviously, he looked up to Billy. And Jerry told me all about the two women who lived beneath us, and one was his Aunt Gloria, the other her friend Faye. But they moved out shortly after I met Jerry.

Late one night, probably after midnight, Jerry and I were sitting out on the porch. There weren't any chairs out there; we always just sat on the 2x4 wood banister. Daddy called down from the top of the stairs to come on in and lock up the door. I ignored him and a minute later he called down again. The third time he called down I yelled back, "I don't want to come in yet, I'll be up in a little while." He called back to me, "I said to come in now!" I replied, "No! Go to bed, I'll be in when I'm good and ready!" (In my mind, I'm wondering what the sudden interest in my life is of what I do? Heck, I stayed out for eight or nine months before when I went to Aunt Emmie's. No one cared! All of us have sat out on that porch many, many times later than this. No one cared! All of us did what we wanted, when we wanted without answering to anyone. Now suddenly Daddy is demanding I come in, what's up with that? Had he ever acted like a parent before now, I probably would be responding differently.) But when I said I'll come in when I'm good and ready, I could hear him bounding down those steps! Jerry took off and went inside his house. Daddy come charging out the door with a hammer in his hand!!! Oh Lord, he done went into shell shock mode! I jumped the banister out onto the sidewalk and ran for my life! Daddy came down the cement stairs off the porch and started chasing me. He was gaining on me so I darted across the street. So did he! I crisscrossed back and forth from the right to the left and back to the right. I was barefooted and I ran using only the balls and toes of my feet so I could run very fast. Each time I zigzagged across the street I could see him still coming and could see that hammer! I was almost up to the project which is probably a half mile or close to it, when I stopped and began trying to spot him. I couldn't see him anywhere. Even looking way down the sidewalks I didn't see him so I'm thinking he's probably hiding behind one of the cars parked all along Broad Street. I very slowly walked back toward the house being very mindful he could jump out from behind a car any second. My heart was beating faster than Little Richard's drummer! I must've drug out that walk out for a good thirty minutes praying he don't hit me with that hammer! When I finally got back to my porch I didn't know if he'd be behind the front door or at the top of the stairs or in my room waiting. I thought about just staying out there all night on the porch alone but that also was a scary thought. I slowly opened the door and was so relieved he wasn't standing there. I very, very slowly made my way up the steps, trying to be as quiet as possible. At the top of the stairs, I placed my hands on the top step and leaned forward trying to see into the hallway on the right and the living room on the left and praying I don't see the silhouette of a man! I ran to my bed and jumped in and covered up my head, still wondering if he was lurking somewhere in the dark. It's a horrible memory I carried with me my whole life. He never mentioned that night to me and I never mentioned it to him.

It's strange how things are meant to be sometimes, Had Jewel not met Lloyd, Judy would have never met her husband Jerry Duncan. Lloyd's mama went out dancing to a place called Curly's and another dance hall called Pleasure Island, both over in SC. Lloyd eventually takes Jewel to those places to dance. While, Lloyd shot pool, Jewel danced with anyone that would dance with her! They invited Judy at some point to go with them and that's where she met Jerry Duncan since he went to those same two places and so did his mama, Juanita. Jerry Duncan began coming to pick Judy up to go dancing and she let me go with them also. I don't know if Dale ever went with them or not but I don't think Joyce ever did. I found it weird that they not only allowed a twelve-year-old in there, but they served me mixed drinks. When Jerry would buy Judy a drink, he bought me one too. I usually drank screwdrivers because I didn't like the taste of liquor of any kind. Judy suggested the screwdriver since it was mostly orange juice with a shot of Vodka and I didn't mind that as much. In those days, at least in the south, if you were old enough to reach the bar, they served you. Jerry Duncan was nice looking and so funny, he kept everyone laughing. He was a roofer in Graniteville and a heck of a nice guy. Judy brought him home and he began staying there all the time. After work he came to our house instead of his folks' place. He hit it off with Daddy. since Daddy loved to cut the fool and make others laugh also. Of course. Mama just loved Jerry; she never met a man she didn't love. But of course, he didn't have anything to do with Mama in that sense. Jerry Duncan eventually met Jerry Morris on the front porch and they became friends. Jerry Duncan was only three years older than Jerry Morris, but he had had a much harder life and had been around the block so to speak much more than Jerry Morris. Jerry Duncan grew up roofing and his daddy had him on the roof as soon as he was old enough to climb a ladder. Soon Jerry Morris was going with us to Curly's and I soon found out he couldn't hold his liquor. He pretty much made a fool of himself every time he went anywhere like that. Seems when he drank alcohol of any kind, he wanted to start a fight with somebody. Problem was, he couldn't fight! Then Jerry Morris got a job in the cotton mill where his mama worked and Lloyd Weeks also worked there. We were all becoming one big sappy-happy family. Jerry Morris would go to Fred Greens after work and shoot pool with Lloyd Weeks. Actually, Lloyd couldn't stand Jerry Morris, but put up with him I guess because of me.

At some point during all the boyfriend saga, a soldier named Don Carney was hanging around. I have no idea how he suddenly appeared in our lives but he was there to see Dale. Maybe just like the dog Brownie, he followed her home one day??? (Oh, and by the way in case you're wondering what happened to Brownie.

She decided to stay there at Welch Lane. She was more attached to Bozo next door, at times literally, than to us. I suppose Brownie figured she had to stay under the house in the dirt and cold and find food for herself anyway, so what does she need with us. And I'll bet she was happy to see the Palmer-Drama move away!)

So, this Don fellow never "dated" any of us, just hung around hoping to eventually! I believe it was Becky Weeks who introduced Don to Dale but Dale says she doesn't have any memory whatsoever of how she met him, so maybe he did simply appear at our house. He had dark hair, stood only about 5'4" with a stocky built. Always wore black dress slacks and a white dress shirt with the sleeves rolled to the forearm. He chained smoked Pall Mall unfiltered cigarettes and drank black coffee almost continuously. He had nicotine-stained teeth to the point they were black in between. Don, who looked every bit of fifty years old, claimed he was a thirty-three-year-old E-4 stationed at Fort Gordon, although he seldom left the house to go to the base. He also said he was from California and had a daughter my age. He had a pink princess phone installed in the small bedroom at our house so he could reach Dale when he was away. Dale on the other hand began to date her future husband, Tom Stallard, whom she met at the No#1 Drive-In, a spot where the teens hung out. A carhop would take your food order as well as your song requests. The local radio station

broadcast live from there and when they played your requested song, you also got to hear your name called out over the car radio.

Or Dale may have met Tom at the Amber House Drive-In or Adams Drive-In. Don Carney had bought Dale a car, it was gorgeous and almost new and it looked just like the one pictured below parked at the Adams drive-in, even the turquoise color was the same. Heck, I bet that's Dale in the car pictured! I don't believe Dale ever drove the car though since she was so young and didn't know how to drive a car yet. But Dale was the bravest of us all, so I also wouldn't put it passed her to drive it. Don finally gave up on Dale and sold the car, I guess.

By now, we're all old enough to make a little money babysitting so we no longer had to go to the city dump or steal bottles or clothes off other people's clothes-lines or go to someone's house hoping to be offered food.

Once Don Carney gave up on winning Dale's affections, he sat his eyes on me, unbeknownst to me. He invited me to go get a bite to eat with him once. It was in the middle of the day; I was hungry and he said we can walk or take the bus. Well, riding on the bus was even more rare than eating in my world, I had only been on a bus once before, so I chose the bus. We walked across the street and up to the corner of Broad and Eve St and waited. There really is another bus every ten minutes! Most of the buses going in that direction are heading downtown so we took the first one that came along. We got off somewhere in the downtown section and walked a half block to a café. We're sitting there waiting on our food and I assumed he'd start in asking me questions about Dale. Like do I think he stands a chance with her, or should he go away and stop trying? I was all ready to say heck yeah, go away but not until the food comes! But mostly he just stared at me! He, in true Don Carney style, took very deep drags off his cigarette and inhale far deeper and longer than anyone I've ever seen! I was thinking, "Shouldn't he need a little air with that smoke?" After we ate our hamburgers and fries, he orders two cups of coffee. I'm thinking, "Okay, here's it comes, the questions about Dale!" He wants to linger and talk but he just stared at me, ddddrag on his cigarette and sipped his coffee. When I became increasingly uncomfortable with his staring and began fidgeting around, he sensed that I guess and he'd look around a little then back to me. This man has to be the most boring man on earth! He doesn't talk, has zero sense of humor, zero personality, and he never laughs at anything anyone else says. If it wasn't for his smoking, I'd have to take his pulse! Then he reached across the table and placed his hand over mine! I immediately withdrew my hand and kept them both in my lap. I didn't say anything but looked away and acted as though I was thoroughly interested in everything the staff was doing. I avoid eye contact with him until he finished his coffee and said let's go. I don't remember what happened after that, I was in shock, I guess. Whether we caught the bus back or walked back or he left and I took the bus back, I don't know. Of course, being the naïve idiot that I was back then, it didn't occur to me until years later, this man is actually a pedophile! He's no doubt a lot older than the thirty-three years he admits to being, as if that wouldn't be bad enough! And yet he wants to hit on girls who aren't even old enough to date yet! I guess he thought he hit the jackpot with five girls whose dad is too sorry to run him off! Maybe Daddy did bring him there. We didn't think so because Don didn't drink and never seemed to talk to Daddy. But heck, Don didn't talk to anybody! He had to smoke to keep from being buried alive. He was the closest thing I've ever seen to a human sloth!

Mama cussed me for everything under the sun because I wouldn't marry Don Carney! I said, "WHAT? MARRY HIM? I wouldn't and couldn't even date him! He's an old man! YOU marry him you like him so much!" She said, "He obviously has money and he's a good man!" ALL men with a wallet were good men in her book. She couldn't stand Jerry Morris, (most people couldn't!) but it would be about as easy to eat puke as to let Don even kiss me let alone marry him!!!! He was so ugly and old!

Chapter 7

The beginning of January 1965 we all got the surprise of our lives when Daddy came in the house just before daybreak waking everyone up. He and his brother Uncle David had come up the backstairs hoping to get in and out again before the police spotted Daddy. I knew we hadn't seen Daddy in days but thought nothing of it. Figured most likely he was in the Stockade again. He was arrested, but was out on bail! But it wasn't simply public intoxication this time. I never knew what he did that he was arrested for. He no longer drove a cab by then and didn't own a car do it wasn't hit and run this time. Whatever it was, Daddy skipped out on the bail and took a Greyhound bus to Indiana. He was in Indiana long enough for his court date to have come and gone so he knew there would be a warrant out on him. Daddy talked Uncle David into driving him to Augusta to get Mama and Dale and Joyce and I and bring us back to Indiana with them. Of course, all this was on Uncle David's dime, who had a wife and four kids and only a single income but this was his brother and he was willing to help Daddy out.

Daddy was rushing us and kept telling us to just grab a few things and let's go. We already had so little and here is Daddy is telling us to leave everything behind. We could only grab a few articles of clothing and Daddy's picture album. All the furniture, dishes, and pots, such as they were, had to be left behind. None of us wanted to go and especially Mama. By this time Jewel was married to Lloyd and had moved out, and Judy was married to Jerry Duncan. Jewel had to come over after we left and get rid of everything.

So here we are, stinking to high heaven, haven't bathe in I don't know how long (due to the cold weather, no coal to build a fire and no hot water) in the back seat of Uncle David's car heading to Indiana. I had never been farther north than Atlanta and Mama had never been farther north than Nashville Tn. We never got to tell anyone goodbye or where we were going (mainly Jerry Morris as far as I was concerned.) They stopped either at a phone booth or in person, can't remember which, to tell Jewel our house is now vacated and she needs to do something with all our stuff.

On the way to Indiana, we stopped at a little roadside café to eat, also on Uncle David's dime. I ordered a burger and it came with sesame seeds on the top bun. Well, I had never seen such a thing. so there I am in all my redneck stupidity having a fit that there's "birdseed" on my bun and I wasn't gonna eat it! Daddy saying, "Wa, wa, Glory, can't you just pick'em off?" I reluctantly agreed, most likely complaining the entire time. Mama who wasn't use to rolling outta bed before noon or one o'clock and certainly not use to eating that early was griping also with her nose all scrunched up. Don't know what she ordered but it certainly put her nose outta joint while she picked at it and murmured. None of us once said, "Thank you Uncle David." Like I said, manners are something we had to learn on our own after we were grown. We didn't stop to eat again all the way to Indiana. When they stopped for gas a couple times, they or Uncle David bought us a cold drink and some crackers. Once there we all unloaded and descended upon Aunt Erma's house. While Uncle David was so soft spoken and shy, his face literally turned red when he spoke in front of others, Aunt Erma was just the opposite. She was a little on the "vociferous" side but so much fun. She almost always started her laugh with sort of a grunting noise from the back of her throat with her mouth closed, then a full all out laugh. She kept us laughing and we just loved her. Well, Mama didn't. Erma could yodel like she was raised in the Swiss Alps rather than Kentucky, and we constantly asked her to yodel, not realizing this ticked off Mama. Evidently Mama was jealous of Aunt Erma and even more so because we bragged on her and enjoyed her company.

With seven kids and four adults to feed, Aunt Erma made grilled cheese sandwiches for everyone, a lot.

She had a large box of Velveeta cheese and that's what she used for the sandwiches. Mama began griping that all "that woman" will feed us is Velveeta cheese instead of being grateful. I thought about how many times we had nothing to eat back home and how we're sitting there eating up their food, contributing nothing and yet Mama is gonna gripe.

Aunt Erma, made us pallets on the floor and I remember thinking, THANK GOD we no longer wet the bed! That would've been so embarrassing if we still did that.

The food, mostly grits, coffee, Velveeta, bread, and butter was getting very low and it had been snowing out for hours. To the point Uncle David could no longer drive since the streets hadn't been plowed. So, Aunt Erma asked some of us kids to walk to the store. She gave us boots to wear and jackets and gloves. Her oldest daughter Angela and Joyce and I headed out to the store. We got as far as the sidewalk and the curb but the snow was so deep that we left our boots buried in the snow when we lifted our feet to take another step. We couldn't even walk in the snow it was so deep. This was January 15, 1965 and it was the biggest snowfall in fifty-five years in Indianapolis!

We thought we had seen snow before but what we had seen, back in Augusta, was the morning dew forming ice crystals on the grass. This was for real snow! We had never seen anything like this before! I don't know what they did about food because every-thing was closed anyway. The whole town was shut down. They had wall to wall carpet which I had never seen before either. I thought rugs were made of lino-leum and had to be nailed down to wood floors but this was soft and fuzzy and disappeared right into the walls! They had these vents on the floor that had heat coming out of 'em! We didn't know where the heat came from, they didn't build a fire and there were no gas heaters to light. Every single room had them vents with heat coming out! All the rooms were warm, not just the living room!

Pretty soon Uncle David got Daddy a job at Stokely-Van Camp canning company. Aunt Erma was insisting we go to church with them. They lived on Fletcher Ave directly across the street from the church they attend-ed, Calvary Tabernacle. But, of course, we didn't own anything to wear to church. What we owned was barely fit to sit home wearing. So, Aunt Erma took us to a used clothing spot, the Goodwill I believe. She paid a quarter for a blue dress for me and a slip and she bought me some shoes also. She also bought clothes for Joyce and Dale. So, the blue dress became my "Sun-day" dress and I wore it every Sunday morning and every Sunday Night. I don't remember what my sisters wore but we loved that church and their choir was so awesome they actually made record albums and sold them. We got saved in that church under the preaching of Pastor Nathaniel Urshan (and Aunt Erma), and although I don't agree 100 percent with all his teachings, he was still a great preacher.

Things were getting a little crowded at Uncle David's house and Daddy had met a man at the canning company who said he had an entire upstairs Daddy could move into with Mama and us three girls, and so we did. I remember when we first arrived and as we were going up the steps, I could see in the man's living room where he had his large floor model TV on a ballgame. I stopped dead in my tracks! It was in color!!! I had never seen a color TV before but to tell you the truth I wasn't impressed. The green grass in the football field was blurred with yellow hues all mixed in and the colors didn't look natural at all. I said as I was climbing the steps, "Well if that's color TV I sure wouldn't want one because that looks stupid." It never occurred to me that the man and his wife and kids could most likely hear what I was saying. None of us had a bit of couth or manners! (Later in life as memories like this come to me, I feel so bad. We were uncivilized, disrespectful, crude, rude, blunt, inconsiderate, unmannered, ill-bred, insensitive bunch of homespun rednecks unleashed on an unsuspecting world!)

That man was nice enough to allow an entire family to move into his home and even went out and bought a bunch of lunchmeats and bread, lettuce, tomatoes, mayonnaise, mustard, chips, and drinks. He

Funny how that side porch seemed so long back then.

invited us down to make us a plate. Standing back and waiting for the man to make his sandwich and watching him put some six pieces of baloney on his sandwich, another sandwich he made himself was chopped ham using half of one package. But… it was HIS dime, HIS food, His kitchen, HIS home. He didn't have to feed us at all! But Mama was going on and on after we all went back upstairs about how much lunchmeat that man used. He still had plenty to feed everyone and we went to bed with full stomachs but that didn't matter. The amount he ate irked Mama to no end! And I wonder if they overheard all the complaining and whining?

We didn't stay in that man's home very long, maybe a couple weeks when daddy rented this house on Harrison Street in Indianapolis.

Mama and Daddy absolutely made up for lost time with their drinking once we moved into our own place. It was like they couldn't wait to get drunk and stay drunk! I mean they stayed drunk! It was no doubt driving them nuts that they couldn't get drunk at Uncle David's and that other man's house. Which just goes to show someone can control it when they have to. But after laying drunk for days and days, they sobered up enough to go get something more to drink in the middle of the night. Daddy came into our bedroom and woke up Joyce and I telling us to get up because we needed to go someplace with them. We couldn't even imagine where they could be going.

We asked them why we had to go too and Daddy said because the cops probably wouldn't arrest them if they had children with them. They walked for blocks and blocks and turned down dark alleys with Joyce and I following along behind them. When we came to one alley they stopped and told us two to stay put because the man might not sell them the moonshine if he sees us kids. So, we stood there at the intersection of those alleys and watch the two of them walk all the way to the end, probably the length of two blocks. (I wonder now why one of them wouldn't stay with us kids and one of them go buy the moonshine.) They made a right turn into what I'm assumed was some-one's backyard and disappeared outta sight. Joyce and I stood there for the longest time and went from un- comfortable to scare. We realized we were in a very bad neighborhood. Two little girls standing in a back alley at 2:00 a.m. stuck out like sore thumbs had anyone been around.

Finally, here they come with a brown paper sack with a quart Mason jar full of moonshine. Daddy told me to carry the bag in case the cops stopped us, they might not ask what's in it if it's carried by a child. The only place Daddy could've found out about the man who made moonshine would've been from a co-worker at that canning plant. Later when I was old enough to reflect on that night from an adult's view-point it saddens me even more how little they valued us kids. I wish I had the forethought back them to "ac-cidently" drop the bag with the glass jar of moonshine in it. No doubt it would've busted and they couldn't have drank that raunchy stuff. But then again, if I had, they probably would have drunk something worse.

Daddy had a 1951 old gray Chrysler that Uncle David helped him get. We had no way of surviving so Dale; at all of fifteen years old and me at all of thirteen took off in Daddy's car and decided to get a job. A girl has to eat after all. We or she rather drove us way out on a very busy highway with about eight lanes to get to a Frisch's Big Boy restaurant. We went in and lied through our teeth about our ages, Dale became eighteen years old and I became sixteen and they hired us both. We were issued uniforms and we reported to work the next day, still driving Daddy's car with no car insurance, no driver's license, and no driver's training. She learned to drive that big old parade float while driving down the road! Dale was a carhop and I was a waitress. The very first week we got paid, we hit that department store named Zayre's. Wow, did we ever love that store. I bought a pair of black slacks and a white blouse, some black flat shoes, and some hairspray. Dale bought herself clothes also. Poor little Joyce, it's a good thing she made friends with a Mexican family down the street or she would've been all alone. She fell in love with a boy named Tony Moralez (I believe was his name) who was too old for her. But she loved hanging out there with him and his sisters and their Mama. There was another girl up the street she hung around with also, don't remember her name. And we met a man named Billy who lived behind us. He didn't really come around much but it was someone to run to for help should a need arise. At least Dale and I knew Joyce had some friends and didn't have to be all alone.

The only stove to cook on in the house was a gas stove and the gas was shut off, so this is where we learned to cook on an upside-down iron and an antique toaster.

Mama and Daddy had dank so much they both had to be hospitalized. First Daddy was rushed to the hospital and was literally dying. Mama was lying there in the bed and she had on a full white slip. She was totally passed out. We noticed there was a wet green spot on her right side coming through her slip. It got bigger and bigger and wetter and wetter. We didn't know what to do, we didn't know if her side had burst open or was oozing from her skin, but either way, we knew she needed medical help. Even as unlearned as we were, we knew that could be gangrene. There was a little store across the street and one of us ran over there and asked them to call an ambulance. So now both of them were in the hospital.

While both Mama and Daddy were in the hospital we girls were very scared at night. Someone was messing around our house and we knew it. There was a transom window above the door and we could see a man looking in at us. We had no phone, no gun, and we knew that old place could mostly likely be broken into easily enough. We could just catch a glimpse of a man's face then he would duck down. This happened for like three nights in a row. On the fourth night we were sitting in the house with it as locked up as we could get it, when we heard loud footsteps on the porch coming toward the door. Our hearts were racing already when someone knocked on the door. One of us asked, "Who is it?" I should've known who it was by the sound of his taps on his shoes. A voice came through the door, "It's Jerry." Lawd, we were so relieved! Just to have a male in the house was comforting to us all. We opened the door and Jerry Morris, along with his cousin Billy Rubin came in. I finally got to meet the infamous Billy Rubin, Jerry's idol. He was one good looking dude! He had blond hair, blue eyes, and a slightly bent nose, but it worked on him. Certainly didn't detract from his looks. One of us asked, "How in the world did yaw get here?" Jerry said they hitched hiked all the way from Augusta, Georgia. I was so happy to see him, not just because we were scared but because it proved he really, really missed me. That's a long way to hitchhike to see a girlfriend unless he wants it to become a more serious relationship.

We no more than began to tell Jerry and Billy someone was looking at us through the transom window when we heard a slight bump on the porch and Billy yelled, "There he is!" He ran and jerked the door open and ran outside just in time to catch a glimpse of white sneakers going over the back fence. It was pitch black back there and Billy being unfamiliar with the yard or fencing or where it goes, decided to just lock the door and come inside. We didn't have a phone or anyway to call the police. Billy Rubin wowed us with his rendition of Thunder Road! All that and the boy could sing! To this day I think of Billy when I hear that song.

After a few days, two detectives showed up at our house in plain clothes. They said we girls had to go with them, that it had been reported we were abandoned children! They put us three girls in an unmarked car and drove just a couple blocks and around a corner and stopped. They waited for a paddy wagon, if you can believe that, to put little kids in and take us to an institution. Well, that sucked. The institution wouldn't even let us smoke. As if life wasn't hard enough, we had already lost our parents and now our cigarettes!

Jerry and Billy just made themselves at home and stayed put. Since they both were sixteen or better the detectives let them alone.

In the institution, we were in a barracks type room with maybe twenty beds in there. They gave us some pj's or a nightgown to sleep in and the next morning we all lined up and went to breakfast. A couple women came over to the long table where about ten of us were seated; they sat a large plate of fried eggs on either end of the table. Each plate had about a dozen eggs on it all stacked on top of one another. As girls grabbed the plates and took a couple eggs off, I noticed the eggs toward the bottom had broken yolks and had all the yolk run out from the weight of the other eggs on top. I guess the hard timers learned to not be last getting their eggs. We didn't care because we didn't plan on being there long enough to learn the ropes. After breakfast, we all had to shower and brush our teeth and get dressed.

Someone came in the room and told us our Daddy was on the phone and to go to the office. Once we were on the phone with Daddy, we forgot all about the administrator who was sitting just across his desk watching and listening to us. Boy we started laying it on thick too, "Daddy, please, please come get us out of this hellhole!" Dale talked to him and then I and then Joyce, we each described the place as all but a torture chamber! We made it sound so horrible so he would come get us ASAP! Daddy kept saying he is trying to get released from the hospital and will be there as soon as he could. We're saying, "Well you better because we don't know how much longer we can take it!" When we hung up the phone the Administrator was looking at us about like this …

We just turned and walked out.

We went back to our barracks where one of the girls had just received a German Chocolate cake from someone who had it delivered. It was her birthday and I guess that was her favorite cake flavor. As in any institution, the other prisoners form little cliques and no outsiders are allowed and we were the new girls. They all pretty much shunned us. The birthday girl cut a few very thin slices of cake and handed them out to a select few. Dale moseyed on over and ask if we could have a slice of cake too. The girl looked at Dale as if she

smelled something foul. She closed the lid on the white box real quick and said, "NO, you cannot!" That was a mistake! A little while later the birthday girl and her friends left the room, leaving the white box sitting on the foot of her bed. That was her second mistake! Dale moseyed on over toward the birthday girl's bed, she opened the box and dug her hands into that cake and torn it up until it looked like mulch out of a garden! Then she walked away saying, "Eat that, Bitch!" Joyce and I didn't get any and we really didn't want any bad enough to lick Dale's fingers. After we left the room a little while later, we could hear yelling coming from the barracks as the birthday girl discovered her cake. But she never said a word to us about it even though I'm sure she guessed the culprit correctly. Of course, Dale could always claim she was looking for the file in the cake so we can all bust outta there.

Within a day or two, Daddy did come get us. Mama was back home too. The doctors said she needed a hysterectomy but she never got one. Daddy on the other hand almost died for sure. He said he was lying there in the hospital bed with all kinds of machines and needles hooked to him. They really did not expect him to make it. They said his blood had crystallized. He said he laid there praying and decided he needed to get on his knees. He said he pulled out needles and tubes and begged God to please allow him to get out of bed and on his knees. He said getting out of that bed was the hardest thing he had ever done. But after he prayed on his knees, he said he began to have a turnaround, began to recover. Supposedly, he has been written up in the medical journals there in Indianapolis Indiana. The doctors told him it was impossible for him to be alive and yet, he was. I have tried to find information on that but with no success so far.

Upon arriving back to the house, I discovered Billy Rubin had left for parts unknown, but Jerry Morris was still there. Daddy had lost his job, his car was repossessed, which meant Dale and I lost our jobs also and we're being evicted. Mama and Daddy just wanted to head back to Georgia. Somehow or the other, Daddy had been in touch with his cousin Teat Jordan who lived in a singlewide trailer in Athens Georgia alone with his daughter Pig, and Teat agreed we could move in there with them. (Oh joy!) Either Mama or Daddy got in touch with Judy and Jerry (Duncan) and asked them to come get us. So, they borrowed our Cousin Roy's car to make the trip. They only got part way and the car tore up; they didn't have the funds to have it towed and repaired so they abandoned it on the side of the road! I don't know how they got the rest of the way to Indianapolis, probably hitchhiked. I do know they met us there at Uncle David's house and they looked tired and angry! Here was fourteen people altogether in Uncle David's house counting his own family and he and Aunt Erma are probably thinking, "No way, not again!!!!" Besides their family of six, there was Mama and Daddy and Dale, Joyce, and I, then Judy and the two Jerry's. Who could blame them for not wanting to accommodate that many people, especially after the unappreciative way Mama behaved the first time? We were all horrible house guests, I'll admit that! We all smoked and just lit up like we were at home. These people didn't smoke or cuss and yet they were subjected to both in their own home! All of us acted like a bunch of ungrateful heathens! Uncle David's car wouldn't make the trip again, and he had already lost work and pay the first time to bring us from Augusta and he had paid for the trip. Here Daddy was broke and couldn't even buy a tank of gasoline. I'm assuming Uncle David talked to friends of theirs, the Baker's, who lived across the street from them concerning the predicament at hand because the Baker's pulled up outside in their Jeep type vehicle and told us all to get in! All except for the men that is. Mr. Baker and his wife, Ollie, and Mama sat up front and Judy, Dale, Joyce, and I sat in the backseat. Mr. Baker acted totally ticked off while ordering everyone around and telling Daddy, "No, no, no, I'm not trying to cram three men in here too! Yaw gonna have to get home the best way you know how. Hitchhike, walk, or crawl, I don't care but I'm not cramming you in my car!" Daddy was scared to hitchhike; he and Mama were avid readers of True Detective magazines and had read horror stories over the years about what has happened to some who hitchhiked and also to some who picked up hitch-hikers. It was cold out again, maybe October or November by now and with the holidays were coming up and I'm sure they all just wanted us gone! Our Uncle and Aunt had gone out of their way to help Daddy and his family make a go of it in Indiana never realizing the severity of their alcoholism! Daddy laid drunk to the point he was hospitalized near death and lost the job Uncle David got for him and the car Uncle David co-signed for. I'm sure Uncle David felt used and abused! Daddy practically begged to be let in that car but Mr. Baker wouldn't budge on that. I was wondering why couldn't Joyce sit in Daddy's lap, I sit in Jerry's lap and Judy sit in her Jerry's lap and put Dale in the very back? There was no trunk, it was inside the vehicle and no one used seatbelts back then. I believe Mr. Baker was mad at Daddy for doing this to his friends Erma and David to begin with. He and his wife had most likely heard all the horror stories and the Palmer drama.

It was freezing outside after dark and Daddy only had a thin jacket, but his brother gave him a long wool dress overcoat to wear while hitching a ride. So we're all off, us in Mr. Baker's car Jeep and Daddy and the two Jerry's on foot.

Later we heard the three of them walked for miles and miles and no one would stop and pick them up. Hours later and now in the dark of night and with the temperature dropping more and more by the minute, they weren't having any luck getting a ride. Finally, Jerry Morris said, "I hitched rides all the way to Indiana from Augusta with no problems, we need to split up! Who in their right mind is gonna pick up three men and with that long coat Ed has on, he looks like a hit man for the mafia! He looks like he could have a shotgun under that coat!" Jerry Duncan agreed and they decided to spit up. Well Jerry Morris went on his way and Jerry Duncan couldn't ditch Daddy no way, no how! Wherever Jerry Duncan went, Daddy went. Jerry Duncan said, "Ed, you gonna have to go on by yourself. You're keeping both of us from getting a ride! I'll wait here until I figure you've walked ahead a mile or so then I'll start walking again." Daddy would not walk away from Jerry! Jerry said it was like trying to get your Siamese twin to go away! Finally, Jerry said,

"Well you're gonna have to pitch that coat or we'll be walking all the way to Georgia!" Daddy finally agreed to dump the coat. He said he like to have froze to death out there. But within a few more passing trucks, they did get a ride and the trucker drove them all the way to Judy and Jerry's door!

Teat Jordan came and got us from Judy's and we stayed in his trailer a short spell. Teat was a self-employed painter and didn't take too kindly to a family of five living off his dime. We were only there maybe three to four weeks and he took us all back to Augusta.

While in Augusta, Jerry Morris and I got married. I was only fourteen years old and he was seventeen. We got married December the 16th, 1965 in McCormick, Georgia. If a legal parent signed for one to be married, they didn't care about the age. But I said I was sixteen just be sure. Mama purely hated Jerry's guts, but she happily signed me away to him. I moved in with Jerry's family and very soon grew to love his mother, Dot. We spent Christmas there, such as it was. Dot cooked a lot of cakes and pies and a feast for dinner. It made a very big impression on me because it was just the opposite of what my mama did for the holidays. And watching the faces of all her other kids light up at the mere sight of all she had prepared made we want to do the same for my future family.

Daddy wasn't having any luck being welcome anywhere it seemed, and he was still afraid of being picked up on the outstanding warrant since he had been gone less than a year. He remembered meeting a contractor named Bo while we were staying in Athens and Bo had told Daddy he had tons of roofing work if he was interested. Daddy had experience roofing with Vincent Griffin and as much as he hated roofing he was considering going back to Athens. And somehow, they did, not sure how they got there but they moved back to Athens.

Jerry Morris turned out to be sorrier than anyone could have predicted and I was already regretting marrying him. Jerry acted as though he adored me and couldn't live without me up and until the Justice of the Peace said, "I now pronounce you man and wife." At that very moment, Jerry turned and walked out leaving me standing there. He never again treated me like I mattered to him, I was his property and that's exactly how he treated me. If I said anything about anything he did, he beat me. He had taken off, leaving me at his mother's, and I had not seen him for days. I didn't know where he was, if or when he was coming back. His mama worked, his daddy worked, his siblings were in school, so there I was, all alone all the time. I was considering leaving when Jerry's mama said she had rented a bigger house way out in the boonies in Martinez, Georgia. It actually used to be a store and was a rather weird layout. She even bought a horse, a lifelong dream of hers. It was a reddish female horse she named Mary, who was pregnant unbeknownst to Dot. Soon she had two horses to feed. Joyce stayed out there in Martinez with us 99.9 percent of the time. Joyce can vouch for Jerry was almost never home. David, Jerry's dad, spent every evening drunk on the sofa grinding his teeth and playing Hank Williams records with tears running down his face; Dot was always working. She was pulling double shifts in the cotton mill trying to afford to feed her horses. Plus slop the hogs at the dinner table every night.

After feeling so abandoned by Jerry, I hocked my wedding ring and Judy and Jerry took us to Athens to stay at Mama and Daddy's, Joyce and Dale came also. I don't remember where they lived but they had acquired a small amount of furniture and kitchen utensils, etc. Most likely with the help of Bo and his wife Marge. We weren't there but a couple days when someone placed an eviction notice on the door to vacate the premises within three days for nonpayment of rent and utilities. We had no way of knowing who the landlord was, had no phone, no money. Judy and Jerry had already gone back to their place and both Mama and Daddy had gotten passed out drunk. We couldn't even ask Mama or Daddy for information. The three of us girls set out to find a place to live within walking distance to where we were. We found a place that was just two or three blocks from a Kroger's grocery store. It was a white house, cannot remember the name of the street. The downstairs was already rented but the main house upstairs was vacant and it came furnished! We knocked on the door of the tenant downstairs and asked the lady about the main part of the house for rent. We told her we needed a place that day! She said she had the keys to upstairs to show it for the landlord and after we gave her a tall story, she evidently believed us and she gave us the keys. She assured us it will be okay. She knew the landlord well and he was super nice. We told her we had just got into town from Augusta and before we could find a place our dad got sick and was at the hospital, our Mama was still in Augusta helping our sister out and would be coming back any day. So, we took off to Kroger's and "borrowed" a grocery cart and started hauling Mama and Daddy's stuff to the new place. Now we had just three days to get THEM sober enough to walk "home." We didn't even know what it rented for, but once Mama and Daddy sobered up they loved the place. It definitely was the best-looking place we had ever lived in.

Soon Judy and Jerry decided to move to Athens also due to Bo having a lot of work and Jerry being a roofer all his life. They also brought Jerry Morris with them and the two Jerry's and Daddy all worked for Bo. Bo and Marge played poker every weekend and Judy and I joined the Jerry's to play poker also. (That way Bo could win back half the wages he paid out that week!)

After just a couple weeks Jerry and I rented our own furnished apartment and so did Judy and Jerry Duncan.

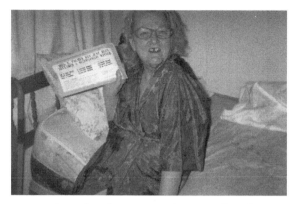

Here's Mama sometime after she went on the warpath and stomped her false teeth, and a couple of the front teeth broke off. But on the bright side, when she put them in her mouth they no longer looked like false teeth.

The two Jerry's got to where they stayed gone every weekend. After work, they just hit the bars and pool halls or wherever. My landlord lived right next door to me and was asking me for the rent money every day. I had no clue where Jerry was or when he'd be back or even if he had any money. If I even asked Jerry where he had been, he would start popping me all in my face until my eye was black and blue and my nose and lips were bleeding, while telling me it's none of my business and who do I think I am to question him. Judy was just as fed up with Jerry Duncan's absence although he never hit her, ever... so we decided to leave them. Dale's boyfriend, Tom Stallard, had become her fiancé and they wrote letters back and forth since he was in the Army and stationed in Germany. She knew that Tom's sister, Donna, lived in Wilmington, Ohio. Dale, she got in touch with Donna to see if we three could come there. We wanted to go someplace where the Jerry's wouldn't look, some place they had no clue we would have a connection to, and we certainly didn't know a living soul in Ohio. So, we contacted Marge and told her our plan and she thought we were just awesome to do that and she was willing to help in any way she could. Judy, Dale, and I got all packed up and Marge picked us up in her car to drive us to the Greyhound bus station. On the way we spotted the two Jerry's walking up the sidewalk, looked like they were heading home, finally. We spotted them before they spotted us and we all ducked down. The Jerry's tried to flag Marge down but she threw her hand up pretending as though she thought they were just waving hello to her. She laughed and laughed about that.

Soon after the three of us had left Athens, Mama and Daddy and Joyce also left and moved back to Augusta. I guess Daddy figured he'd been gone from there long enough he wouldn't be arrested. Back in Augusta, Joyce made friends with a girl name Patsy Favors and the two of them hung out at a pool hall called Doc Mills place pretty much all the time. She said they frequently just sit outside the place and smoked and talked. One day as the two of them were sitting there, a fire truck rode by and there was Mama standing on the back of it waving and yelling, "Hey, Joyce, look at me!" Joyce was so embarrassed and just said, "What the hell?" Mama was half lubed up and had walked somewhere to get more

Mike

Samuel

Bryan

Chuck

to drink and on her way back she had stopped at the fire station that was just up the street from Doc Mills place, and hounded the firemen for a ride on their truck. She wouldn't let up and being the good ole boys that they were, they finally obliged her.

It was also while being in Doc Mills place that the door opened and in walks a guy Joyce has never seen before. She looked up and thought, "Oh my God!" Picture a young George Clooney, that's how good-looking Richard Crawford was! He had just returned from Vietnam and his mom dropped him off at his favorite pool hall. Eventually the two of them were married.

In Ohio, I got a job as a carhop, met my present husband, and filed for divorce from Jerry a year later. The next time I saw Jerry Morris, briefly, I was about thirty years old, had a REAL husband and three sons. We have been married now for fifty-three years and have seven grandchildren and four great grandchildren and two more one the way. He is a wonderful man and I thank God for him. If I hadn't been running away from Jerry, I would not have met Bryan.

Jerry went on to remarry four more times and wasn't married at the time of his death. He died at his mama's home at the age of fifty-six from liver disease.

Judy went back to Jerry Duncan; they bought a home in SC and had two daughters and three grandchildren and two great grandchildren. They were married forty-eight years. They are both deceased.

Dale married Tom when he returned from Germany. They had a daughter and a son. Tom became an alcoholic and Dale divorced him and a couple years later married Jerry's brother, Daniel Duncan, and they have a son together and five grandchildren and two great grandkids. They were married forty-three years. Daniel has since deceased.

Joyce married the little boy who watched us five girls run away from Ms. Coopers Home. Richard Crawford. They have two daughters and five grandchildren and three great grandkids. She divorced Richard who also became an alcoholic and she married Wayne Roberson. They have been happily married for thirty-one years.

Jewel and Lloyd are still married and been together for fifty-eight years. They had four children and at least eight grandkids and about that many great grandkids. They have always lived in Georgia.

It's funny how all five of us girls have obsessions which no doubt stems from our childhood. Jewel is obsessed with towels and pj's; always having new ones put away she's never used yet. Judy was obsessed with groceries, spending hundreds every week at the grocery store. Dale is obsessed with nice sheets and comforters; I am obsessed and buy too many shoes, underwear, pj's and groceries and Joyce is obsessed with buying too many towels and pj's also like Jewel. I have bagged up and carried sixty-five pairs of shoes out at one time to give away while leaving another sixty-seven pairs in my closet. I have done that twice in the past six years. Same with never worn bras, bags of 'em given away. And with food, I have to throw out outdated canned and boxed goods because they expire before I can use them all.

Closing Thoughts

Most folks, I would imagine, reflect back on their childhood as adults and may have some awakening moments. Mine seem to all come in my thirties, like realizing the small can of brains Mama put in scrambled eggs actually were "Hog Brains," Mare-ree was Marie and Lil' Genia was Eugenia. Who knew? And the reoccurring nightmare was a memory of me as a baby in a crib, looking through the bars and crying. And it was Mama who came bounding in and leaned over me and did something to hurt me bad enough to cause the reoccurring nightmare. And once that awareness hit me, the nightmare has never returned. But I'll remember this next particular day for the rest of my life. I was thirty-seven years old, standing in my kitchen in Conyers, Georgia putting dishes away.

My husband was at work and my sons were in school. My dad's words, "I have five beautiful daughters" ran through my mind for whatever reason. And for the first time I realized what he was actually saying. It washed over me like a bucket of cold water. I began to cry because that was the only compliment I had ever heard from one of my parents, and I just realized it was not a compliment at all. But mostly because of what he was willing to trade for a drink of alcohol. He put our safety at risk when it was his job to protect us.

I had always felt it was easier to forgive Daddy than Mama because he didn't hit us or cuss us or tell us he wished we were never born and he hates us like Mama did, but suddenly I'm faced with the realization he didn't love us any more than she did either. We only thought he did. I picked up the phone and called two of my sisters, Dale and Joyce but didn't get an answer from either. I reluctantly called Judy. Reluctant because Judy purely hated Daddy already and also because I just knew she was going to say, "You just now figured that out, I've always known that!" I would've bet money on that would be her response, but it wasn't. When I told her the only time Daddy said that was when he brought men in the house, there was total silence... you could've heard a pin drop for probably thirty seconds! Then in a very low voice she said, "I be damn." We talked for a while, but I just wanted off the phone to be alone with my thoughts. The very words, the only words that made me feel good about my daddy for thirty-seven years now just brings heartache and pain. I hate remembering those words now....

Daddy did apologize to us kids for the way we were raised and making us do without and go hungry so many times. He said, "If none of yaw ever spoke to me again, I couldn't blame ya." Well at least that was something.

Personally, I struggled even more with forgiving Mama who unlike Daddy, has never apologized for anything she had done or had not done where we were concerned. In fact (when she was sober) she would stand and tell visitors right in front of us that she made sure we were in the house by eleven each night and if we weren't she'd come find us. That she put three meals a day on the table and if we didn't eat it that was our own fault. AND she actually said that with a straight face! She honestly thought she could convince others she was a good Mama, a sober cleaning, cooking, clothes washing, march her kids to school with a hot breakfast in their stomach kind of Mama and we were a bunch of lying ungrateful spoiled brats. I was grown the first time I witnessed her tell someone that. I wondered, right after I picked my jaw up off the floor, just how many people has she told that?

Yep, SHE was the star of the show right up till the end.

As one final thought, I'd like to say that both my parents are in heaven now. I believe that because my sister Joyce led Mama into the sinner's prayer not too long before she passed away, sober, in August of 2001. And Daddy constantly asked for forgiveness and cried out to God. He died from fear we believe, fearing the coming of the year 2000. He was so convinced that at one minute after midnight come December 31, 1999 the whole world would erupt into total chaos. Television news stations were constantly broadcasting that no one knows if every computer would suddenly shut down or not since there was no dates pass 1999 programmed into them. They said the power grids may go out, which means no one can pump gas, no cash registers would work, no social security checks being deposited, no way to get your money out of the bank if you had any and no way to spend it if you take it out early. They perpetuated the fear on very TV station. Daddy, who had already had by-pass surgery before, couldn't handle it. He was literally scared to death. He died sober at home on December 1, 1999.

I believe in heaven. I'll get to meet the people God intended them to be all along.

Epilogue

I realize there are thousands of children a lot more abused than the Palmer girls ever were. I praise God that none of us ever was raped or suffered sexual abuse or was ever sent to the hospital with broken bones. Although we endured malnutrition and a lot of verbal and emotional abuse, as well as being hit with a police belt. I have learned to forgive my parents, we all have. Forgiveness is important because it frees you; it is for you more than for the ones who hurt you. If you are a survivor of abusive parents then give thanks to God you survived and refuse to continue the suffering in your heart and your mind. Realize you deserve to be loved and treated well regardless of what your parents did or said to you. My parents were broken people who were also products of broken people, who were products of broken people, and on and on. We can decide to carry that brokenness into the next generations or we can heal in our spirits and hearts and give our children the nurturing and loving childhood we never had. It is a choice

ALL parents teach their children good parenting skills by example, either what to do or what not to do.

Thank you for reading my story, God bless.